WORD FROM POUSTINIA

by
ROBERT WILD

Priest of Madonna House

DIMENSION BOOKS

DENVILLE, NEW JERSEY

Published by Dimension Books
Denville, New Jersey 07834

ISBN 0-87193-066-8

To my Madonna House family through whose love
I am daily graced with the gift of solitude

INTRODUCTION

I live in one of the poustinias at Madonna House. As many people know from Catherine Doherty's book *Poustinia,* the word means "desert" in Russian. A poustinia is a small cabin where people ordinarily go for a day of prayer and fasting, though some, like myself, live there several days a week as a way of life.

One of the thrusts of the poustinia spirituality is to share with others what you hear the Lord speaking to you in solitude. Frequently, when people return to the main house after making a poustinia, they will ring the bell in the dining room and say, "The Lord be with you." All answer, "And also with you." Then the person shares a "word" from his or her poustinia day. The message of the poustinia is "for others," whether prayer or penance. This sharing of the "word" emphasizes and incarnates the fact that what happens there is not for yourself alone but for others as well.

This book contains "words" that I heard the Lord speaking to me. Many of them were shared at the Eucharist in the form of homilies; some were originally in the form of letters sent to my Madonna House family; some few were written for publication elsewhere; still others were jotted down for no particular reason. Writing from the poustinia is one of my ways of preaching the good news of Jesus, the exalted and unmerited privilege for which I was ordained.

God's word does not come to us (at least, it does not come to me) in any orderly, systematized way. His word flows from life, and life is not systematized, at least, it shouldn't be. I have really tried to group these writings around certain themes to make a more orderly presentation for the reader, but no thematic approach seemed to work. Why make a pretense of order when there really isn't any? When God plants a forest, he scatters the seeds at random. All kinds of trees grow haphazardly, here, there, and everywhere. When we plant a forest, we plant the trees in rows! Both forests are beautiful, but different.

The order of this book is of the first kind; I pray that it is also beautiful. It contains "words" that came to me in the poustinia and which I desired to share with others.

The Lord Jesus said it very succinctly: We do not live on bread alone but on God's word. As I reflect in this book, *"logos,"* "word," in the time of Jesus, meant precisely "meaning." We really live by the meaning we can attach to our loves, our hopes, and our dreams. For Christians, Jesus is our "Meaning." Every other true word is simply another aspect of the mystery of Jesus. May these words help to enrich your life as they have enriched mine.

These words were born in the desert, in the poustinia. The desert may seem like a very "roundabout way" of fostering Christ's work on earth. I begin with a biblical reflection on the place the desert should have in each of our lives.

Special thanks to Marian Heiberger for transcribing tapes, and Mrs. Bess Shanahan for typing the manuscript.

Madonna House, Combermere, Ont.
May, 1978

The Desert: 'Roundabout' Way

The wilderness or desert is one of the major themes of the bible. "The wilderness was the decisive period in Israel's primeval history."[1] If we consider the history of God's dealings with Israel as normative for our own personal relationship with Yahweh, then an understanding and a reliving of what happened to Israel in the desert is crucial to our own life with God. Have we ever given much serious thought to the idea that a desert experience may be part of revelation for each one of us, the revelation of an experience and a situation in the life of God's people which each one of us somehow must share? Although there are four different words used to describe wilderness or desert in the bible, the one most frequently used refers to the sojourn of Israel after its exodus from Egypt.

God's people were eager, we presume, to get out of Egypt, with all its back-breaking work and everything that accompanies the condition of slavery. But not too long after their departure, the difficulties of Egypt looked very good compared to the situation they now found themselves in. We too are so at home and comfortable with our sicknesses of all kinds that we'd rather stay with them than start on the road to health. At least we can manage in our state of illness. We know who we are and even though we are sick we are surviving. We feel some of our diseases slipping away from us as we enter the desert, and the prospect of health frightens us. The world of total purification might be more terrifying than Egypt. "The wilderness is

---

1. Quotations in this section are from *Christ In the Wilderness*, by Ulrich W. Mauser (London: SCM Press, 1963).

the place that threatens the very existence of Yahweh's chosen people."

Why is the desert threatening? It is threatening because it is the place which lacks all the supports which we believe are necessary for our existence. Ordinary dialogue with many people is absent. Other people are one of our main supports for reassuring us that we are not alone in the universe. We give lip service to the fact that there is Another present in our lives, the Person of all persons. But in the desert we are actually challenged to put all our trust in this Other. We must now put our lives where our pious thoughts gave us the illusion of being "at home" with God. We must learn to say from experience, "Lord, You are people and presence and company enough for me." It is in the desert where that sentence no longer is beautiful poetry but a matter of life and death.

The desert is threatening because of the silence and the absence of activity normally associated with "living." We matter-of-factly equate noise and activity with living. When something is happening, or better, when we are making something happen, we are reassured that we are not nothing. In the desert we are challenged to experience that simply to be is the greatest and most fundamental activity of which we are capable. We are challenged to experience whether we can live meaningfully at this most basic level. We are challenged to say (again, not as mere pious phrases, but as utter reality), "Lord, You are my life." Ordinarily we say this and then get on with other things just in case the Lord is not sufficient.

If we are willing to experience the loss of these superficial aspects of existence for a while, then God can manifest his power. "The wilderness . . . is also the stage which brightly illumines God's power and readiness to dispel the threat.'' God actually upholds us all the time by his power. But there are dimensions of realizing this power which we can foster by concretely relinquishing the superficial supports of Egypt. Will we allow the conscious realization of his power to enter us by and through a desert experience? Yahweh knows that the desert can be this place of discovery of his power and his presence, and that is why he leads us into it.

Our radical dependence on God is not an occasional event, occurring perhaps once a week. It is constant. This is a hard lesson to learn and to live out. The teaching of this lesson was part of Yahweh's desert discipline: ''Yahweh helps his people in the wilderness from day to day. Israel is not permitted to live in security lest she forget that she is utterly dependent on her God.'' The time in the desert is a time of experiencing constant dependence. Our temptation is to call on God from time to time when life gets shaky; for the rest we are under the illusion of coasting on our own. The temptation of the people in the desert was to continue this pseudo-existence by demanding large amounts of bread so that they would not be wondering all night whether God would feed them on the morrow.

But God does not give overflowing storehouses of superficial food in the desert. He fed his people only one day at a time. Outside the desert, where the illusion of supporting ourselves is normal, planning and filling granaries is part of life. We rest secure in our storehouses. We turn to God occasionally to thank him for the abundance and maybe panic a bit when they start to diminish. In the desert the storehouses are always empty. It is a time for learning total dependence, minute by minute.

The disorientation and confusion of the desert is preparatory to deeper encounters. "(Several) decisive events take place in the wilderness which are once and for all decisive and normative for the religious life of Israel. The first of these crucial events is the revelation of God's name."

Each person is a little universe of his own, and each person experiences reality in a slightly different way than the next person. This is also true of our experience and our relationship with God. Although we all give him the same name—God—he is actually special to each one of us and in some way we have our own special name for him—what he is or means *for us*. In the desert, when the supports of our personal world are removed, a new name for God emerges and is revealed to us. Just as in the history of Israel God's name actually changed as they experienced him in different cultures and situations, so in our personal lives, God's name, in a way, is constantly changing, or ought to. Depending on the kinds of egypts we are trying to leave behind, God will reveal himself to us in the desert as "He-who-gives-me-courage," or as "He-who-upholds-me-in-darkness," or as "He-who-is-personal-center-of-everything." In the desert God will reveal his name to us, just as he revealed it to Moses (Ex. 3:6).

By this revelation of his name, God makes the desert the place where personal relationship begins. Introduction, introducing ourselves, is the first step to conversation. "It becomes possible to say that Israel's religious life as a partner of Yahweh begins in the wilderness. The desert is the place of God's initial and fundamental revelation to his people." The desert is, therefore, a covenant-making place and a law-giving place. It's a strange paradox to say that although Israel left Egypt as a people they were not yet a people, a unity, with a common bond and a common God. In the desert God put order into their chaos. Out of a multitude of disunited tribes he formed a people. Their unity came about by all of them facing together the mountain of God and pledging their loyalty and their lives.

It is similar with us. We enter the desert presumably as a whole person and yet we quickly discover our fragmentation. We too are like a loose federation of warring tribes. Through the nakedness of a desert experience God wishes to unify us, to experience the basic laws of our life with him, to allow us to experience these laws as sources of life. Through a kind of unification, a vague and general "God" becomes "my God," and the universal "Word to mankind" becomes "God's Word to me." The wilderness was the "womb of the religion of the Old Testament." Could it be that such must be the case for each one of us, a desert experience where personal covenant becomes a reality which unifies our fragmentation?

Total dependence is a hard lesson to learn. Because the desert is without any "visible means of support," it is the place where our lack of trust and faith stand out most glaringly. "The desert is also the scene of Israel's sin which comes to light at once." God, we quickly discover, is not enough for us. We rejoiced for a little while as he fed us, as he revealed his new name, as he disclosed to us the basic laws of life. But we forget easily. Soon we begin to murmur and hanker after the life of Egypt. We can stand just so much reality. The great temptation periodically in the desert is to *get out*.

"Israel makes an attempt to shorten the time of waiting, seeking to escape the desert before God allows them to do so." This is our temptation too, to "shorten the time," to make our timetable God's timetable, and to arrange our stay in the desert just long enough to make it interesting without endangering our normal supports. Until the Lord comes in all his fullness, we need some idol to hold onto. Outside the desert substitutes for God remain more firm. In the desert the only image the Lord will allow us is his *changing name,* as we have the courage to allow his presence more and more to enter our lives. But such a shifting relationship is too illusive for us. We need some static idols, some visible images to rest in a while before we continue on our journey. "The revelation of the name of God is forgotten in exchange for a visible image."

Thomas Merton once wrote that many people leave Egypt but very few enter the Promised Land. We sense the need to leave Egypt, but after we get in the desert we are not so sure. The delights of the desert can only be revealed by crossing it and by trusting in the Lord.

There is a beautiful passage in Exodus on how delicately the Lord deals with us in this journey. "When Pharaoh had let the people go, God did not let them take the road to the land of the Philistines, although that was the nearest way. God thought that the prospect of fighting would make the people lose heart and turn back to Egypt. Instead, God led the people by the roundabout way of the wilderness to the Sea of Reeds" (13:17-18). In Yahweh's travel plans for us, the desert often seems like a waste of time and truly a roundabout way of getting to the heart of the matter. We would like to strike straight ahead and cut the Philistines down, get to the Promised Land and be done with it. Why all this desert stuff? In the Lord's mind, it seems that before we can fight the philistines in our lives and in our society, we must learn the art of life's warfare at its deepest level. And what is the plan of battle in the wilderness? Paradox of paradoxes, it is to keep still and let Yahweh fight for us: "Moses answered the people: 'Have no fear! Stand firm, and you will see what Yahweh will do to save you today: the Egyptians you see today you will never see again. *Yahweh will do the fighting for you: you have only to keep still*' " (Ex. 14:13-14).

In the desert we learn how to live in the rhythm of the well-springs of Life if we can allow all our superficial supports to fall by the wayside as we journey. In the desert that most nagging of all questions of man—"Is Yahweh with us or not" (Ex. 17:7)—will be experienced and answered with a depth and clarity we never dreamed possible: "Now I know that Yahweh is greater than all the gods" (Ex. 18:12).

Our "Religious" Age!

What "ism" did Jesus fight against most of his life? It doesn't seem to have been atheism or secularism, or even communism! He seemed to have the greatest trouble with the "ism" of Pharisaism.

Basically, that's bad faith. It's hypocrisy. It's saying one thing and doing another. The religion of the Jews was not bad—Jesus never repudiated the Jewish faith he was born in. But he had a lot of critical things to say about some of the leaders of that religion.

In our situation today, it seems to be almost the other way around. In our day there appears to be a lot of hankering after religion, a lot of religious fads, and in many of these, I believe, there is good faith: People are sincerely searching for God. But there's a lot of *bad religion*.

We tend to think that religion is good. Religion, the religious quest, is one of the most powerful forces in man; but if religion is misdirected, it can be a very disastrous thing. It is a lesson of history that our faith can be misplaced. In the name of religion, men have done terrible things.

I would just like to quote briefly from the New York Times: "In the dingy back room of an abandoned music store, fourteen young men and women in brightly colored psychedelic robes sit cross-legged on the floor and chant Sanskrit to the tinkling of tiny triangles, while the perfume and smoke of incense floats about their nodding heads." The article continues, "People have got ads in newspapers announcing that they have found the true way to God through group therapies, Synanon games, flying saucers, astral trips, psycho-drama, mathematical computations, IBM machines and schemes of every conceivable sort. It is truly a religious generation."

We know that there is also some bad faith in the religious quest. We know that there are some people who consort with positive evil, satanic cults and very dangerous things. But I do believe that there is a wide area of people sincerely searching for God, but in all kinds of bizarre ways! What are some of the criteria by which to judge real religion?

We know that any religion worthy of the name must regard *God as central*—the living God has to be its center. I read in an article in "Time" that a new religion was started. Ten thousand people belong to it already and a portrait of the founder of the cult was above the altar! Any religion, in the true sense of the word, must have the living God as its center. The center can't be the "way of enlightenment'' or anything else except the living God.

Another aspect of much bad religion today is the disregard for the suffering neighbor, for which any religion worthy of the name has to be concerned. But today there is a lot of pietism which is simply an involvement in religious experience for its own sake. It's a kind of religious quest that merely feeds on emotions and religious experience, with complete disregard for suffering humanity. And that's bad religion.

Sometimes some of these religious quests are in the name of Christ, but they only take part of Christ, they only take part of the scriptures, or parts of the Bible. There are many such religious sects today. They want Jesus but they don't want his divinity, or they want the Holy Spirit but they don't want the Church, they want community but they don't want authority. They pick and choose in the Bible and take certain things, and somehow their religious quest doesn't have a wholeness about it. On a more superficial level perhaps, we know that any kind of true religion has to make or form true people, whole people. Religion has something to do with making us whole, complete. There are many religious quests today from which people emerge very weird, very strange, obnoxious, or impossible to live with, inhuman. What kind of religious quest are they on?

It is your great privilege, and mine, to be part of what we believe is the true religion, the true religion of Christ. That's not to say that in our own lives we don't have these faults too, of pietism, and lack of concern for the neighbor. We too are a mixture of good and bad. But by the grace of God we pray that there is more of the face of Christ that shines in us than our own inadequacies. We pray that his mercy might be greater than our own perversity. And we pray that the people who come searching for what religion really is all about, may somehow see in us the answer to their quest.

The Most Amazing Journey

What is the most amazing journey you've ever taken? Did you know that every year our little planet travels about 600,000,000 miles around the sun! Imagine if you could sit for a few years at the Palomar telescope and watch this incredible journey every year. What sights! What a display of shooting stars and comets! And yet, this journey around the sun is like a walk around the block compared to the journey of our own galaxy through space. We'd like to know how fast and how far we're going, but there's no way of measuring our speed or distance because everything else is moving! Yes, everything in the universe is on an immense journey.

But there is a journey still more incredible. The astronauts tell us that even the trip back and forth to the moon gets "boring" after awhile! You know what the most incredible journey is? It's the journey of the conscious, willing, loving person into God. St. John tells us that God is love. The most incredible journey is this journey into the Ocean of love.

Imagine a person saying, "But I don't want to go around the sun again!" There's nothing we can really do about it. In the same way, we are headed into God, one way or another. Little by little, every year the little space ship which is ourself is moving towards eternity. So many people live and try to journey with their emergency brakes on! Inside they want to stop, yet they are moving all the time. It's the journey into God for which we were created. Imagine the interior sights of moving ever more deeply into the marvels of God's life with us! What sights, what explosions of grace and adventures! May you give yourselves completely to this journey! Will it, accept it, do not wish you were not traveling! We have no choice, really—like going around the sun. We do have a choice on how we shall travel—willingly, with a spirit of adventure, or dragged against our will. One way or another, we are going. May you accept the journey and take off your brakes!

"When I Saw Him, I Fell at His Feet as Though Dead" (Rev. 1,17).

Whenever we are really in the presence of the Divine mystery, our whole being, interiorly and exteriorly, desires to be flat on its face! (As the Hasidim say, in that position there is no danger of falling!) Poor, sinful creatures that we are, we are torn by two seemingly opposing tendencies: to face God, and to ef-face ourselves in his presence. Made in his image, we desire to look into his face unashamedly, with pure eyes, for we know this is the whole purpose of our creation. Yet, the holiness and awesomeness of God, and our own sins, propel us to face away from him, to the earth from which we came. Let us see what light scripture throws upon our falling down in God's presence.

There is the scene in the Garden of Olives when Jesus is about to be apprehended by the soldiers. In response to Jesus' question, "Whom do you seek?" they answered, "Jesus of Nazareth." "Jesus said to them, 'I am he.' When he said to them, 'I am he,' they drew back and fell to the ground" (John 18,5-6). Father Raymond Brown says

that John intends the "*I am*" here as the divine name, and
that the falling down is in reaction to it. Also, in this in-
stance, the adversaries of Jesus fall in confusion; they are
not "effacing" themselves out of reverence and awe and
love.

The physical falling down of the guards is simply the ex-
ternal manifestation of what happens to the hostile areas
of our hearts when we encounter the Word of God. "He
shall smite this earth with the rod of his mouth, and with
the breath of his lips he shall slay the wicked" (Is. 11,4).
When we ask the Lord for a text of scripture, and our eyes
fall on such readings, our tendency is to keep on searching!
Such words are hard to take! We fall on our faces to hide
from the secret places in our hearts.

In the Book of Daniel we read of Daniel and the King
falling on their faces before God as a result of the revelation of a mystery. "A great God has made known to the
King what shall be hereafter. Then King Nebuchadnezzar
fell upon his face, and did homage to Daniel . . . "
(2,45-46). "When I, Daniel, had seen the vision, I sought
to understand it; and there stood before me one having the
appearance of a man; and when he came near I was
frightened and fell upon my face" (8,15-17).

Sometimes, when the Word of God enters our hearts, it
is not precisely the awesomeness of God, nor shame at our
sins, that prostrates our souls. What "ef-faces" us is the
revelation of a secret about ourselves, God, or life. Suddenly, our whole interior world is flooded with light and
we say, "Oh, now I see, now I understand." In the same
moment we are aware that such light did not come from
our own efforts. Then, we take off our shoes and bow to
the ground, for the Lord is present.

In the Book of Revelation we have still another experience of God which prostrates our souls. "And all the angels stood around the throne and around the elders and the four living creatures, and they fell on their faces before the throne and worshiped God, saying, "Amen! Blessing and glory and wisdom and thanksgiving and honor and power and might be to our God forever and ever! Amen!" (7,11-12). I presume this figure applies to men as well as angels.

In heaven, all sin and shame will be gone. In the light of God's face all mysteries will be revealed. Yet, we will still be propelled to effacement before the awesomeness of God himself. This effacement, then, is not simply due to sin or ignorance. It is a deep and perhaps the most profound longing in our souls: to shield our faces from the face of God and by that act see him as clearly as it is possible for us to see.

When God chooses to manifest himself in some special prophetic word or action, it is always powerful, and we cannot remain indifferent to it. God's presence comes at us head on and confronts us with so much truth that all we can do is be silent, bow our heads, and in our hearts fall to our knees. And this is true whether we accept God's word or not. In the former case, our interior prostration will be life-giving. In the latter, it will be a judgment upon us. But "my word shall not return to me void."

While we could specify various levels of God's coming to us, we basically experience two dimensions, consolation and judgment. This is so because we are not yet wholly light in the Lord. We all carry in us at one and the same time the truth about our beauty and about our ugliness. And God comes to us, now revealing one part, now another. When we read or have experiences of God in our lives that say, "It is I who answer and look after you" (Hosea 14,8), our hearts rejoice, jump up and down, and prostrate all at the same time! But when we experience God saying to us, "Your love is like a morning cloud, like the dew that goes early away" (6,4), then we feel more like the soldiers who were knocked over!

I think a sign of a mature relationship with God is being able to fall down in a life-giving way in the presence of both these approaches of God. One who is always bowing before the God of consolation, or always bent low before the God of judgment, has created an idol, and does not encounter the living God. For we are at one and the same time soldiers in the garden, kings before unknown dreams, and angels around the throne. We are and will be all these people together until God in his graciousness removes the tears and the veils from our eyes.

And just as we should be interiorly prostrate when receiving God's word, so should we be prostrate before our brothers and sisters when giving it. What an awesome thing to speak God's word to one another! Should we not be bowed down before one another!

If we ourselves are prostrate before the God of consolation and judgment, our own word will reflect both these dimensions. Some people only speak the word of consolation. After a while it begins to border on sentimentality and doesn't ring true. Some people only speak the word of criticism and judgment; after a while we turn them off too because their word is simply crushing us to the ground and they rub our noses in it. But if someone will rise from before the living God and speak words of both comfort *and* criticism to us, then, ah, we hear the truth sing in our hearts. That person has spoken to both the soldier and the angel within.

A terrible thought, isn't it, that there is a part of our hearts that wants to apprehend Jesus and silence him! God in his mercy knocks us down to bring us to our senses. What a glorious thought, on the other hand, that part of us sings and falls on its face, saying, "Blessing and glory and wisdom and thanksgiving to our God forever and ever." For creatures such as we are, there is no other way to see God's face as it really is than to efface ourselves in complete adoration. If we are faithful to his Word, one day the soldier in us will disappear completely, and the *"I am"* of Jesus will stir in us nothing but total praise. We will all feel the hand of Jesus upon us and hear him say, "Fear not, *I am* the first and last, and the living one; I died, and behold *I am* alive forever more" (Rev. 1,18). Then, in an eternal rhythm of rising and falling, we shall see him face to face with every motion of our being.

God As Life Together

The religious question could be phrased very simply: Are we alone in the universe or not? Is there a presence, a power, behind, in, through things, behind, in, through ourselves? Or are we really alone? Every answer to that question implies a kind of faith.

Of those people who believe that there is a God, a Power, a Presence at work in creation, there is a great variety of understandings of how much we can know about this God. If you asked Buddha about God, he would just smile. He wouldn't even try to explain the smile! He would just say that the proper study of man is man and about

God one can know nothing. If you asked the Jew about God, he would say, "Listen, Israel, the Lord your God is one God." He would say something of what Moses said: "Was there ever a people so fortunate as to hear the voice of the living God speaking out of the burning bush?"

The Jewish people believe that God can really communicate with man, that we can really know something about him. Yes, these are human words and symbols, and yes, they are totally inadequate. There is so much about God that we can't know and won't know. But the Jewish person has a tradition: "Was there ever a people to whom God has spoken as God has spoken to us?"

Finally, if you asked a Christian about God, he would say, "Glory be to the Father and to the Son and to the Holy Spirit." The Christian says that the mystery of God involves a unity of a trinity of persons. Our friends, the atheists and the agnostics, would say that this is quite presumptuous: "What do we know about God?" We say that many of the things that Jesus told us are really quite "unreasonable"—that's why we believe them! Was there ever a man who said: "I and the Father are one?" That's incredible! Was there ever a man who said: "He who sees me, sees the Father." That's really incredible! And was there ever a man who said: "No one has seen God, but the Son in the bosom of the Father has revealed him." Was there anyone who ever spoke like that?

So it is our faith that the deep mysteries of God's own life have been revealed to us. That he is a communion of Father, Son and Holy Spirit. It's very important how we think about God. If we are honest, sincere, authentic people, we become like the gods we worship—whether they're material or spiritual gods. We become like the gods we bow down to.

We know that our understanding of God can become an abstraction. We can say that we love him, and in our life do something quite different. Martin Luther King, on Sunday mornings, used to walk up and down the streets of Birmingham, Alabama, watching people coming in and out of church: Christians. He used to say to himself: "To whom are they praying, and what God are they worshiping here?" Of course, people would say that they are worshiping the Father of Our Lord Jesus Christ. But there was something missing in their understanding of the Godhead and their living it out: the two were not exactly the same! I'd like to quote from one of the documents of the Second Vatican Council:

> The Lord Jesus when he prayed to the Father that all be one as he is one, opened vistas closed to human reason, for he implied a certain likeness between the union of divine persons and the union of God's sons in truth and charity.

This likeness reveals that man cannot fully find himself except through a sincere gift of himself. My brothers and sisters, our belief in the Trinity means that we believe that *all* life ought to be a communion of persons. It means that we believe that life cannot be good after all unless through a gift of ourselves to one another. Every time that we say, "Glory be to the Father and to the Son and to the Holy Spirit," we are expressing our faith that there is nothing in the universe that is isolated; that everything is and ought to be dynamically related to everything else; especially people to other people.

There are many ways that we can think of our baptismal consecration: we think of it as dying and rising with Christ; we think of it as conversion. But it is also a dedication of ourselves to the fact that *all life is life together in the Trinity*. Jesus said: "Go and baptize everybody in the name of the Father and of the Son and of the Holy Spirit." He was saying: "Go and baptize and commit yourself to the deepest truth of reality—*that life is life together.*"

So every time that we bow and say, "Glory be to the Father and the Son and the Holy Spirit,"—if it is not to be just an abstraction, an idea in our heads—we have to live out in our lives the fact that we are consecrated to be creators of human community. Every time that we say, "Glory be to the Father and to the Son and to the Holy Spirit," we are consecrating ourselves to the fact that we are creators of friendship among people. Every time that we say that, we are asking God to help us break out of our isolation, to help us to reach out and create friends.

The Music of the Spheres

One week the Lord taught me something about simplicity and prayer. It all began with a story I read about one of the early Greek philosopher-scientists of the sixth century, Pythagoras.

"One day, as he passed a blacksmith's shop, his ear was attracted by the apparently regular musical intervals of the sounds that came from the anvil. Finding that the hammers were of different weights, he concluded that tones depend upon numerical ratios. Since all bodies roving in space produce sounds, whose pitch depends upon the size and speed of the body, then each planet in its orbit about the earth makes a sound proportioned to its rapidity of translation, which in turn rises with its distance from the earth; and these diverse notes constitute a harmony or 'music of the spheres.' Someone asked him why then we cannot hear this 'music.' He said: 'We never hear it because we hear it all the time.' "

I'm no scientist, so I don't know exactly where Pythagoras' theory of music in the spheres stands right now, but his answer, "We never hear it because we hear it all the time," was a phrase which stayed with me throughout the days, and which the Lord used to teach me a few things.

It is the realities which are with us all the time that we often fail to see. The eldest son in the "Story of the Prodigal Son" did not realize his father's love for him because it was so constant. We do not pay attention to the page on which words are written, though it is the page which allows the letters to stand out. As we go about our day, we do not think of the air we breathe because it is ever-present, yet without it nothing else would happen. We think more of where we're walking than of the miracle of being able to walk. We think more of *what* we or others say than of the wonder of being able to communicate at all. And when we *think,* we pay more attention to the thoughts than to the astounding organ of the brain itself.

Perhaps simplicity has something to do with being able to hear this constant background music of our lives, the music of God's constant gifts which are so ever-present that we only infrequently pay attention to them. Perhaps simplicity means not being so caught up in our own words, thoughts, projects, comings and goings, that we are unable to hear this music.

At prayer one night, with Pythagoras' answer still floating around in my mind, I wondered how God speaks to us. Prayer is supposed to be a conversation. It occurred to me that the reason why I often did not hear God speaking to me was because he was speaking all the time. God was speaking in his gifts to me—he was present in his gifts. My very body standing here in prayer was God speaking to me. My brain that I was using to think about him was his speaking to me. The air I was breathing, the gift of solitude, my vocation at Madonna House—God was present and speaking in all the realities so close to me that their very closeness made them almost invisible.

It's a wonderful way of praying sometime, simply to realize the gift of your mind and body, that even before you prostrate or stand or speak or think, these ever-present gifts of God's love are yours. God is too close to us! Even as we conjure up beautiful thoughts and aspirations, God wondrously keeps our body and brain in order so that we can praise and thank him.

Perhaps one result of our Christian discipline should be a greater capacity to hear the "music of the spheres." Christian freedom might have something to do with the ability, with the help of Christ, "to distance ourselves" more and more from our own music so that we might be able to hear the background music of God. There are so many marvelous realities always present; we are not present to them.

Pythagoras didn't say that the music was so loud or so many octaves above us that we couldn't hear it. He said we hear it all the time. I remember that one night as I returned to my poustinia, I saw the sky ablaze with stars. There was no wind, no sound, yet (this was before I knew about the music of the spheres), it sounded as if some music were coming from the stars. Similarly, when you're in a place of absolute silence you seem to hear the silence.

Our own "music" is the discordant notes of our hearts which are out of tune with the Lord's music. For we too, as we follow the tune of the Spirit of Jesus within us, are part of God's symphony. Listen to Clement of Alexandria as he speaks about Jesus the "New Song": "See what power the new song has! He has structured the whole universe musically, and the discord of elements he has brought together in an ordered symphony so that the whole Cosmos is for him in harmony. By his Holy Spirit he tunes the Cosmos, especially this little cosmos, man, mind and body; and he sings to God with this many-voiced instrument.

He accompanies his song with the instrument of man—'For thou art to me a harp, a flute and a temple'—a harp by the unity of parts in one whole; a flute by the living breath; a temple by thy reason; a harp that rings in harmony; a flute that breathes melody; a temple that is the Lord's house."

May we more and more disregard our own discordant music so that the Spirit of Jesus may play upon our hearts—so that we may be able to hear God's music of the spheres coming to us through all of creation.

Our Family As Guru

Sometimes, when I come out of the poustinia, before anyone gets a chance to ask *me* for a word, I say: "Has the community any word *for me* this week!"

I believe there is also a word of the Lord in the community as well as in the poustinia. During the past few weeks I've been working with the community a little more, especially with our guests; I asked the Lord if there was any special thing he'd like to tell me about my relationship with them. He replied "The family is the guru."

We all know the instructions the Fathers of the desert used to give the new arrivals: "Do what I do." If the novices were faithful in doing what the master did, the Lord would instruct them in that very doing.

Our family is like a collective guru. I think that if the people here with us for only a few days or weeks would just do what we do—live our rhythm of work, prayer, hospitality, recreation—the Lord will teach them many things. He will instruct them in the very doing if their hearts are open and at peace.

When a person first comes to Madonna House the experience is really overwhelming. There is plenty of spiritual food on which to feed. I often think of Madonna House as a kind of "spiritual smorgasbord." Our daily life is the table spread with a variety of foods. But it is the Lord who is the Chief Servant. He knows exactly where each one of our guests is in his or her life with him. Our task is to assist him as best we can.

Thus, there is no need for us to try to say the right thing or rush in and save somebody before he leaves in a few days! God is doing so much with our guests that perhaps most of all we need a kind of reverential fear lest we get in the Lord's way.

The other day I came across a beautiful explanation of the word "temple." The *templum* originally was a space in the sky which the augurers had marked off and which they consulted to discern the will of the gods. Then, the physical building was called the *templum,* either because it was the place where people met to receive the message from the gods, or because this *templum* was the physical pattern of the *templum* in the heavens.

Now, we are the temple of the Holy Spirit, the temple of Christ, the temple of the Father. We try to mirror in our lives the vision Jesus has for us. Also, our community life reflects the visions of countless seers down through the ages, topped off with the vision of Catherine herself which she has seen in the Lord.

All people need to do who come to us for their short stays is to live out every day this vision of the temple. It is here, in our temple. It is beautiful and wholesome and holy. Even if they don't understand it at all, God will instruct them as they live it.

The word "guru" means one who dispels confusion. Our family is the guru. The vision of Jesus will be manifested to our guests as they share with us the rhythm of our lives. He, through our lives which make up his temple, will dispel their confusion.

The Lord Is My Hiding Place

Hiding is a universal human experience. Remember the game of "hide-and-go-seek" we used to play as children? Of course, we don't play such games any more—or do we?

The first experience of hiding we come across in the scriptures is the man and woman hiding from God in the garden. The author of this account of creation was a profound psychologist. Try to recall your experience of not having done your homework when you came to class. As it came time for recitation, the teacher scanned the class,

looking for someone to call on. Even though you were ex-
posed to full view, there was an interior hiding going on.
You would have liked to have had something to hide
behind. It's hard to hide out in the open! Or remember a
time you actually did something wrong, and how you hid
from your mom or dad. You and I hide from the face of
the Lord every time we hear his voice calling us to greater
responsibility and we say, like the child who didn't do his
homework, "Who, me?" We "make pretend" God
doesn't see us. We play games with him.

A second kind of hiding is found in the gospel. After
Jesus healed someone he told him not to mention it to
anyone. That's a kind of hiding, a good kind. People tend-
ed to misunderstand the meaning of his signs and wonders,
so he asked them to hide them from others.

Jesus also taught us that when we do good work we
should not let our left hand know what the right is doing.
One of the deeper aspects of our Christian life is to try
sometime to help others without desiring *even deep down*
that anyone find out! Oh, often we do things secretly for
others. No one is around, but we wouldn't be put out if
someone found out about it! There is a kind of hiding of
our good deeds that purifies our life with God. We should
try, like Jesus, to do good deeds as an offering to the
Father rather than for personal glory.

There is the line in the Psalms, "The Lord is my hiding
place." Isn't that beautiful! We all have our favorite
places to go when we want to "get away from it all." (My
favorite hiding place was under the dining room table.)
Wouldn't it be a complete reversal of the experience
described in the creation story if instead of hiding from
God we arrived at the point where *he became our hiding*

place? What a wonderful way to express a return to God by describing him as our hiding place! "I have not spoken from some hiding place, but I have spoken openly to you." God does not play hide-and-seek with us. He speaks openly to us; he is not ashamed of anything he has said or done in our regard. So let us pray for each other that we may stop playing games with God (except that we might truly make him our favorite hiding place!).

A Carthusian Day

Catherine wrote a letter recently on the theme of monotony in daily life. Then, as she often does when meditating on this theme, she carried our minds to the Carpenter at Nazareth and to the mystery of his very ordinary life there. While reflecting on this particular letter I had a flashback to my life in the Carthusians. I don't think the regularity and the sameness of a Carthusian day could be matched by anything short of solitary confinement in a prison! Not even ordinary prison life, for I'm sure convicts have more diversion than was customary in a Carthusian cell.

When I say you do "exactly the same thing every day," I mean *exactly*. You're supposed to sleep in the same posture, rise immediately when the bell downstairs is sounded. Since you've slept with most of your clothes on, dressing doesn't take too long. You proceed immediately to your small oratory where you greet Our Lady by reciting the morning hours of her Little Office. At one time I was able to recite, by heart and in Latin, the whole Office of Our Lady, so regular is it.

Then you light your little kerosene lamp (it's midnight,

the beginning of the "Carthusian night"), and proceed to the main chapel where the chanting of the night Office takes place. Return to cell. Another hour of Our Lady's Office. Perhaps a brief time of meditation: then, after about three hours, back to bed again. It's about 3:00 A.M.

Rise about 7:00 A.M. Prime and mental prayer in your cell. Proceed to Church for community Mass. Private Masses of the priests afterwards. Return to cell. Another hour (Terce), privately, spiritual reading and some manual labor. This manual labor was either working in one's small garden, or in the workshop downstairs, sawing wood or turning something on a wood lathe.

11:30: Sext, dinner, free time for relaxation, which meant an hour for artwork or something like that. 2:00 P.M., None (study of the Order or Philosophy if one were going on to the priesthood), and manual labor.

4:00 P.M.: Vespers, spiritual reading, then Vespers in community. Once a week the whole Office of the Dead was also recited after Vespers. 5:30 P.M., supper, prayer, spiritual reading. Then around 7:00 Compline and so to bed. At midnight you rise for the night Office again and the whole cycle begins once more.

This routine is lived without talking to anyone else all week, without leaving one's cell, except for a weekly recreation on Monday afternoons when we all go for a walk together for several hours outside the monastic enclosure. In the Novitiate, the novices meet once a week, and the Novice Master might pop in once in a while during the week also. Other than those times, there is no break in the schedule, and you never speak to anyone. There are no newspapers, no radios, no T.V.s, and letters are received twice a year. During the two years I was there I only heard two pieces of news: Kennedy's election, and (I think) the Russian Sputnik going up.

What I wish to witness to here is that, in such a life, I experienced something of the mystery of Nazareth, something of what Catherine was speaking about in her letter. The Carthusian life is built on the faith understanding that the all-holy God is present in the minutest aspect and activity of everyday life, but that most people are so distracted from him that they cannot see him there, cannot meet him there. I witness to you that such a routine became the vehicle for an incredible freedom to concentrate one's whole attention and love on the Lord. The routine became the source of life because now the inner man was freed to meet the God who is always present, who is always totally there to speak to us and to commune with us. Monks live this routine every day of their lives, but the externals no longer matter. They have been led to the God who is always present, and it is him they are seeking. The externals are indifferent.

The mystic insight of the ages is that the Infinite is present in every particular moment and place—in a rose, in my every thought. The Infinite. The Source and the Goal of all my loving and striving, the ultimate meaning of my life. Where is he? He's right here. Totally present, totally waiting, totally embracing. He waits for us to stop our wanderings and to meet him in the present moment.

These "wanderings" of course are not necessarily physical, though they can be. God's will may take us here and there. Very few people can live like Carthusians. Yet the principle is the same. Our lives are totally adequate to find the Lord. We need not be concerned about useless wanderings in order to find him. The task now is the journey inward: to see whatever routine we are in as life-giving and as freeing us to meet the Lord who is always present.

This is not monastic spirituality only. This is the mystery of Nazareth. This is the mystery available to everyone if only we have the courage to enter upon the incredible journey. We have all begun that journey. The keys to its completion are *faith* that God is always present, and the *love* to overcome the obstacles in us to enter more deeply into that presence.

I remember a fundamental conviction I had from the Lord all the while I was in the Carthusians. It was this: God keeps me in existence, so there is no reason why I should not be able to survive by being completely alone. It was the conviction that one didn't really need anything else but God to exist. I lived on the principle that any fear, any pull within me to hold onto anything somehow had to be burned away, let go, so I could be upheld by God alone. The Talmud says, "A tree in the desert is still a tree." I love that saying. Everywhere is our center, because God is everywhere and we can come to him there. A simplicity of life can free us from surface living and be the means for plunging us into the God who is always present.

Remember and Never Forget

There is a story from Buber's *Tales of the Hasidim* that is very instructive.

A certain rabbi had celebrated the Passover with great pomp and ceremony. He was very pleased with himself as he retired to his room and sat at his desk. Suddenly he heard a voice saying, "The Passover of Hakkim the tailor was much more pleasing to me than yours!"

Needless to say, the rabbi was quite shaken, and he ordered that this tailor be brought to him.

Hakkim came in and sat down. There was a long pause of silence (Hakkim was obviously a little drunk). Then the rabbi asked: "Are you Hakkim the tailor?" "Yes," Hakkim said. "Did you celebrate the Passover tonight?" Another long pause. "Answer me, did you celebrate the Passover?" the rabbi asked again.

Sheepishly, Hakkim looked up and said: "You see, Rabbi, it was like this. You know that we are not supposed to drink wine for seven days after Passover. So, since I was having my troubles, I thought I'd sort of drink a little more the seven days *before* Passover. Well, I drank too much. When it came time for Passover I was fast asleep and my wife came in and said: 'What kind of a Jew are you! Why aren't you celebrating Passover like everybody else?'

"So I got up, staggered over to a table, sat down, and poured myself a glass of wine. Then, I simply said, 'God, you saved our people once from the land of Egypt. God, you are very powerful and, you know what, I believe God, that you'll do it again! God, I drink to you!' Then I went back to sleep."

By now we are all familiar with the notion of the healing of memories, that there are traces in us of hurts and wounds that need to be impregnated with the healing presence of Jesus and his Holy Spirit. There are also present in our memory banks *all the wonderful things that God has done for us.* These are like sacramental chalices holding the seeds and waters of hope within us.

Often, in the Bible, one aspect of sin is simply the forgetfulness of God, of his presence, of his past favors and mercies. The prophets are forever *reminding* the people not to forget what God did for them. Paul tells us that the Scriptures are all about hoping, about a people who, when they were down and out, hoped in God and were not disappointed.

My brothers and sisters, perhaps we should pray over each other sometimes *to be healed of our forgetfulness of God's past wonders and mercies in our lives.* Hakkim's Passover was more pleasing to God because he believed with his whole heart in the very essence of the feast: that God had saved his people in the past and that he would do it again. What greater compliment can we give God than to trust in his promises?

This calling to mind God's mercies and wonders is not in any way living in the past. Those experiences are in us and part of us—*are us,* in a sense—and to recall them is simply to reflect on ourselves in the light of all God has done for us. We can do more: from our present stance of faith, we can now see God's presence and action in certain of life's happenings where before we did not recognize his involvement. All this should be grounds for hope: God helped us once and he will help us again. To hope is to believe in the presence of Someone who is more creative and ingenious than we are.

Jesus said that we don't know who God is if we lose hope. We have to stop projecting our own ways of acting on God. We have to remember that his view of possibilities is greater than ours. Above all, we simply have to remember, remember all he has done for us, remember all the wonderful mercies present in our memory traces. Those are just as much a part of us as the hurts and the wounds.

Yes, let us pray for each other that we have a healing of memories, and never forget his many mercies to all of us all throughout our lives.

"You may say in your heart, 'These nations outnumber me; how shall I be able to dispossess them?' Do not be afraid of them: remember how Yahweh your God dealt with Pharaoh and all Egypt, the great ordeals your own eyes have seen, the signs and wonders, the mighty hand and outstretched arm with which Yahweh your God has brought you out. So will Yahweh deal with all the people whom you fear to face" (Deut. 7, 17-19).

Compassion, Key to God's Heart

In Is. 62, 1-5 we see the vision that God has for mankind. People today talk about the absence of God, but in the first line of the reading, God says, "I will not be silent. I will not be silent about my plans for Israel, for the human race." God looks down on the human race and he sees all the divisions. He sees the struggles in Northern Ireland. He sees the division between the Russians and the Chinese, between the North Americans and the South Americans. He sees our own divisions, divisions between the blacks and the whites. And God says, "All these people can *still* be united . . . ."

Do we really believe God? I mean, way down deep in our hearts, as we are working for unity, do we believe that all these warring factions can become one family and sit down together at one table?

The very first step in our working for unity is for us to *really believe that.* In our own life, think of the persons we have the most difficulty with. Do we believe that God can make us one? If we don't, St. Paul says we make God a liar, because he has raised Jesus from the dead and made him Lord and Victor over all the divisions. God said: "My dream is to make you all one." Jesus prayed for that, "Father, that they may be one." Therefore it must be possible. Do we really, actually believe it is possible?

The theme for Christian Unity one year was "Endurance in Hope." In the second line of the reading, this theme appears. The Lord says, "About Jerusalem *I will not grow weary.*" To work towards unity is to hope, not to give up. God does not give up on us. Jesus does not give up on us, and we cannot give up on others or ourselves, however deep our divisions are. Sometimes in our relationships we adopt the approach of the U.N. with its peace-keeping force. It doesn't solve the real problem. Both sides are there, poised for attack, and the U.N. has to walk up and down and in between to keep the peace. Sometimes we think that is the best we can do: a holding action but no real unity. That is not God's vision. God's dream is for the bride and the bridegroom to be totally one, and we must believe that ourselves.

In our struggle for unity, we say to God: "We can't do it! There are so many different kinds of people. Who can unite them all?" And the Lord says: "There are all kinds of services to be done, working in all sorts of different ways in different people." We say to God, "God, there is a lack of wisdom on earth. Nobody seems to know which way to go, how to become one." And the Lord replies, "One may have the gift of preaching with wisdom given him by the Spirit; another may have the gift of instruction given him by the same Spirit." We despair, "Lord, we have so many wounds from our past and our present. Who can heal them?" The Lord answers, "Another has the gift of healing.'' We protest, ''Lord, we don't have any faith.'' The Lord says, ''Another has the gift of faith given by the same Spirit.'' God knows that we can't achieve this unity by our own power, so he pours out his gifts. He wants to pour out upon us all these gifts: wisdom, instruction, miracles of healing. Do you need anything? Ask him for it! Do you need faith? Ask him for it! You need healing? Ask for it! The Lord wants to pour these out on us. The same Spirit working in all to bring us all together.

I prayed myself, asking ''Lord, what is the key to this unity in our own hearts? What is the key to it all?'' And he replied, ''Something like Mary at the wedding feast of Cana: *She was concerned for others.*'' It was always the women who had to prepare meals and keep food flowing at such a gathering.

The wedding was just getting started and all of a sudden—people must have been pretty thirsty, traveling all day—the wine was gone and they had no more. If you had been in charge of the feast, you would have been nervous too. The Lord said to me: ''The key to unity is concern for the Body: When you forget yourself and you become concerned for the needs and unity of other people.'' That is what Mary did. Mary was sitting there and suddenly noticed that things were starting to break up. She was concerned for the party. And through her concern for the body, her concern that people stay happy and have a good time, she stepped out. She could have embarrassed the host and the hostess doing that. Maybe it wasn't her place to do anything. But it didn't matter. She went to Jesus and she said, ''They don't have any more wine.'' It is that kind of prayer, the prayer of total concern for others, that works miracles. Jesus said: ''I haven't planned it this way. I

haven't really planned to move out yet. It is not my time."
We don't know the length of that whole conversation.
Mary smiled and walked away, and said, "Do whatever he
tells you." She had this perfect confidence that God knew
the situation. Sometimes when we pray we think God is not
aware of what is happening and we have to inform him of
the crisis! Mary knew that Jesus could do something if he
wanted to, so she just left it completely in his hands:
"Jesus, they don't have any wine." Jesus, in our own
lives, wants to change all the water of our disunities into
wine. And he can do it. That day, he made a couple hundred gallons. He was lavish. What a party that must have
been!

That same kind of power is available to us; Jesus wants
to do the same thing for us. We say, "The needs are too
great and the wounds are too deep, and I don't know if
even God can do it." Jesus says, "Fill up all the water
jugs. If you only have six, fill them up. If you have ten, fill
them up. If you have a hundred, fill them up. Now, serve it
out." There was enough for everybody. And his disciples
believed in him. He manifested his glory, and they believed
in him.

Jesus manifests to us also every day these miracles in our
lives. We have to recognize and then see that the water is
changed into wine, and let our faith increase every day and
recognize what he is doing. He is more powerful than all
the divisions in our lives, in our community, among our
nations.

So let us then pray for faith in the power of God to
destroy all our fears, to change all the waters of our divisions into the wine of unity and life.

God As a Baby

Around Christmas time one year I was thinking about God as a Baby. If we look at the wonders of nature and see how beautiful nature is, we say, "That kind of beauty must be in God in some magnificent degree." And if we have an experience of power—Niagara Falls—we say that that power must be in God to some nth degree.

So too, when we look at a baby. I think it's true to say that the essence of "babyness, babyhood," is in God also. Three characteristics of a baby came to me.

The first one is attractiveness (at least when he's not crying, or wet, or throwing up!). How to define attractiveness? Someone draws us because he or she is delightful, lovable, pleasant, and these qualities resonate in us and stir life within us. We experience a flow of life. God himself must be the essence of attractiveness.

Another characteristic of a baby is that it is completely *helpless*. I thought to myself that in some deep way, God, in his relationship to us, at some moments in our lives, is completely helpless. Each one of us is at a certain point in his or her life with God, and God in that area has really done everything that he can do short of making robots out of us. God himself arrives at a point of helplessness, complete helplessness. He tells us, "The next move is *yours*. *You* have to reach out to *me* now." God is helpless because if he takes one more step he might destroy our freedom. He is helpless because he made us free and now he must wait.

A third characteristic of a baby—or our relationship to him anyhow—is that a baby is always somehow at the *center of our attention.* The mother and father who really love that child are somehow always thinking about the baby. Whatever they're doing, the baby is present in their consciousness. And I think too, in our life with the Lord, we want to acquire that kind of awareness in our lives. We never want to forget him in some deep space of our being. He's always there, he's always the Center.

Sometimes, my brothers and sisters, when I'm standing in prayer in the solitude of the night, I begin to be afraid. Then I think of the Baby. I don't think of the Judge. I don't think of the Lawgiver. I think of Jesus as a Baby and then peace comes again and I can stand there a little bit longer.

The next time that happens to you in any aspect of your life with God, ask yourself, what God are you thinking of? Think of the Baby. How can one be afraid of a baby?

So, very simply, I offer you this meditation: God is a Baby. These "baby" characteristics do not exhaust God's character, of course. But neither do those of Judge, Lover, King or any other analogy. When we're overwhelmed by his love, we think of the Lover. So, if ever you're overwhelmed by fear, think of the Baby. How can you be afraid of a Baby?

Meaning Became Flesh

The famous passage in Eph. 1, 3-14 is magnificent. I was struck not so much by any one line or thought but by the sweeping power of the passage as a whole. It seemed to me that it was like a powerful searchlight, a light which illumines our whole life. It reveals God's plan for us, the story of our lives. I would like to share some thoughts with you about the healing power of light.

When I walk back to the poustinia at night, I ordinarily do not have a light, so there is some groping and stumbling. One night I walked into another poustinia by mistake! When I finally found mine and turned on the light, there was a sigh of relief. Light and home.

Sometimes when we are traveling to a city and we don't know exactly where we are going, we become all tense and anxious until we get the right directions. Then, oh what a sigh of relief when we see the right street and the right house. Then there was the old experience (old for some of us!) of not knowing the right answers on an important exam. We started to sweat a little, our stomachs were tied up in knots. Then the answers came and all was well. We relaxed all over. What a joy is caused in our whole being when light floods into our physical or interior eyes! On the other hand, isn't it a common experience that ignorance causes confusion, tension, and anxieties throughout our whole psyche? We are tied up in knots inside because we can't see.

What if a person can see no light or meaning in his *life*? What does the word "mean" mean? Well, among other things, it means to be able to see how a part fits into the whole. We want to know how one thing is connected with another. To see relationships is to understand. Why are world visions like Marxism and the vision of Teilhard so attractive and powerful? One reason is that they offer a vision of the whole, at least as these men understood it, and this sweep of things has a tremendous power because it helps people see the meaning of things, connections, and how their own lives "fit into" everything.

In that passage in Ephesians, God has revealed the meaning of our lives: "Before the world was made, he chose us, chose us in Christ, to be holy and spotless, and to live in love in his presence." He has revealed, in Jesus, his plan for us, our story. He has revealed the secrets of his heart from all eternity, the mystery of our adoption as his children through Jesus' death and resurrection.

Many of you have heard of Dr. Victor Frankl, who, as a result of his experiences in the death camps, elaborated a whole method of psychotherapy around the concept of meaning. He said that only those persons survived the camps who had a reason, a purpose for living. He called his approach "logo-therapy," "meaning-therapy."

When the early Christians said that the *logos* became flesh, *logos* for them signified precisely "meaning." When the Greek philosophers discovered the meaning of things, they used the term *logos.* Thus, one way to read St. John's Gospel is to say "Meaning itself became flesh." *What Everything Means* has come to our earth. If you want to know the meaning of life, look at Jesus. He is *Meaning become flesh.*

My brothers and sisters, there are so many thoughts in us that are darkness and not light. It is blasphemous to entertain for one second the thought that God does not love us when he has sent his Son and revealed to us in him the whole plan of our salvation. It is blasphemous to think that we are not lovable when Love himself came and walked among us. It is blasphemous to think we are stumbling around in the dark.

We must *fast* from all such thoughts, discipline the kind of thoughts we entertain. Our emotions follow our thoughts. If we allow dark thoughts to be in us, darkness will spread through our whole person. And this is why we must *feast* on the Word of God, feast on the light of the gospel. We feast on everything else—food, conversation. We must learn to feast on the Word of God which will dispel the darkness and illumine our hearts with the healing light of Christ.

Jesus gave us power over all spirits, spirits around us and in us, any force which tries to darken our souls and separate us from the Father. There are many lights in the world which are false, many lights in us which are false. We must force out the darkness with the light, expose the dark corners to the light. Jesus is the light, and we know him and possess him.

Yes, we know the meaning of life, the story of God's plan. Just think: what all the philosophers and great thinkers of the world have sought and are seeking, we know! We know the meaning of life, and we are sure. So don't ever walk around saying, "My life is meaningless. I'm in the dark. I don't know where I'm going." Again, blasphemous thoughts! We *do* know. The Father has revealed it to us in Jesus. "He has let us know the mystery of his purpose, the hidden plan he so kindly made in Christ from the beginning."

Truly, blessed be the Father of our Lord Jesus Christ who has blessed us with every spiritual blessing in Christ! Blessed be the Father who has revealed to us the meaning of our lives—blessed be he for allowing Meaning itself, the divine Logos, to dwell among us!

A Little Rule for Life

How succinct and profound each sentence of the gospel is! If we lived just one of them deeply, entirely, the Lord would reign in us. In the few lines of Lk 9, 43-45, we have an entire plan of life—three attitudes which, if we carried them deeply in our hearts, would allow us to live the gospel.

"Everyone was in admiration for all that he did." We are to live in constant awe and admiration of Jesus, think about him, stand marveling at his words of life and his deeds. To always live in admiration of Jesus—this must be a constant attitude for us.

"Have these words constantly in your minds: The Son of man is going to be handed over into the power of men." We must always keep in mind also the sign of the cross which is placed over every follower of Jesus. He says, "Don't ever forget: Anyone who follows me will encounter pain and opposition within him and around him." Just imagine, Jesus who came to save men, must say to us: "Remember, I will be handed over into *men's* hands." We can almost hear the anguish of his heart: "Men for whom I came will betray me and put me to death." Thus the second attitude, along with admiration for Jesus, must be a remembrance of the cross. He told us beforehand not to be scandalized when it came.

Thirdly, his apostles did not understand what he said and they were afraid to ask. Did they not understand *because* they were afraid to ask? I think so. One thing the Lord has taught me in the poustinia is that he will really give me whatever I ask for. It is becoming less and less of a mystery just how God wants me to come to him. The problem now is my courage to really ask for the things he reveals to me. We are, like the apostles, *afraid to ask*. We need the courage to ask. The disciples did not understand because they were afraid to ask: they ran from the crucifixion because they were afraid to ask. They didn't keep their eyes on Jesus because they were afraid.

Mary is the perfect example of these three attitudes. How full of admiration she must have been for what her son was doing! Yet, she had been told of the sword that would pierce her own heart. All through Jesus' life, she must have also beheld the sign of the cross. But she was never afraid to ask. Whether at Cana or any other time, she was never afraid to ask Jesus for light, strength or courage. Yes, these three attitudes are really sufficient for all our needs.

Three Themes

There are three themes in the world now after the Resurrection, three basic statements. In some way I think everything else could be seen as a variation on them.

One theme is that Jesus is alive, and that God loves us, and all glory and honor and adoration is due to the Lamb who died for our sins. It sings that our guilt is no more and sins are forgiven for anyone who wants to admit them and believe in the Lord Jesus. God loves us absolutely, unconditionally, without reservations, and his love is available to all. This is the psalm that the birds are singing. It's a psalm that we too sing in our hearts and long to sing more completely every day.

There is another theme, a discordant note, echoing throughout creation. It goes like this: "Do not preach in his name. You are forbidden to mention the name of Jesus. He is not alive. The guilt of his death is on us. You still have your sins and you will never be able to conquer them. The darkness in your heart is for real, and you will just have to live with it." That lie is shot through our institutions, our culture, our past; it is part of our own hearts. It is the lie perpetrated by Satan himself. He knows that he has lost the grace of God, and he doesn't want anyone else to acquire it or to get it back. "Do not preach in his name." There is an area in our hearts where we feel that the name of Jesus would be powerful and healing. But we hear voices all around us: "Do not preach in his name. We forbid you."

The third voice in creation is the voice of Jesus. Jesus is risen from the dead, walking along with us on the road of life. He says, "Do you love me? Do you love *me*?" It is the eternal question, and we know he asks it of us every day of our lives in all those areas where we think we will never be able to overcome, never be able to conquer. Jesus says, "Do you love *me*? I don't ask what *you* can do. I don't ask how great a faith *you* have. Do you love *me*? Do you trust *me*? Do you believe in *me*, not yourself?" That is the question.

There are parts of us that say with Peter, "Yes, Lord, you know we believe. We do." And we really do. But there are parts of us that say, "Do not preach in his name." In the simplest terms, that is the eternal struggle now after the Resurrection. God is absolutely for us; and there are powers that are absolutely against us. How *we* answer the question, "Do you love Jesus?" decides the issue for us.

Let's make no mistake about it: every time that question comes up it is important—there are *no little things,* no little nos! In professional hockey every move is important. Every turn of the blade and every swipe of the hockey stick has consequences. If a player is off by a millimeter, it can mean the game. Let us make no mistake about it: Jesus has made us professionals of life. There are no small things, there are no small involvements, no small decisions, there is no small anything. His Holy Spirit in us witnesses to his Resurrection. The Holy Spirit in us witnesses that God does love us, that our sins are forgiven. We dare not answer that question, "Do you love me?" in any other way.

The Nazareth Way To God

We probably do not think enough of Nazareth. Most of the time we meditate on the public life of Jesus which was, after all, only a very small part of his total life.

If we had been in Nazareth and knew who Jesus was, sometime around his eighteenth or nineteenth birthday we might have said something like this: "Well, you're going on twenty soon. Don't you think it's about time that you started to move out a little, maybe preach in the evenings after work or something?" I imagine that Jesus would have answered something like this: "No. I have come to be man, simply man. Most people on earth will spend their whole lives simply working from dawn till dusk. I want to help them realize that they can come to my Father in this way, by simply working, caring for their families, accomplishing the tasks of life that God has entrusted to them."

What a mystery is this life of work of the Son of God! For thirty or more years Jesus worked all day, filling orders, paying his bills, going to the store, talking with his neighbors, keeping his Mother company, resting at night in preparation for the next day's work. He simply wanted to be a man.

Most people will never be able to do great things, like

traveling around the world preaching the gospel. Most people are not "getting ready" for some great mission in life. Their daily work is their mission. Jesus wanted all of us to have faith that we could come to his Father by being faithful to the work entrusted to us. But we must work in faith, as Jesus said in the Gospel: "This is the work of God. That you believe." Our work cannot become an obsession, the end-all and be-all of our lives. We must work in such a way that it leads us to the Father, taking care that we are not over-anxious in our work.

There is a beautiful legend among the Jews. They say that at each moment of the world's history there are thirty just people (according to some rabbis thirty-five!) and these people, by the purity of their lives, uphold the whole earth. It is only a legend, of course, but I believe that most of these people would be simple working people, people whose hearts have become so purified by simply working and doing daily things required of them that they became completely unaware of how close they were to God. So let us pray for one another that we always have a great respect for the dignity of work and a great faithfulness to the work God has entrusted to us. And let us have a deep and profound respect for the hard-working people of the earth whom we meet. Who knows, he or she may be one of the just ones who are holding up the whole earth!

"Don't Trust Me!"

The words are not mine, my brothers and sisters, they are from the Scriptures: "A curse on the man who puts his trust in man, who relies on the things of the flesh, whose heart turns from Yahweh" (Jer. 17:5).

"Such texts are destructive," we murmur to ourselves. "How could we live together if we didn't trust one another? All the latest books tell us to trust one another, to be a trusting person, to present a trusting presence so that people can find acceptance in us, etc., etc. Jeremiah was probably a misfit anyhow!"

When I read these words an insight came to me so suddenly and so clearly that I felt sure I was meant to share it with you. The Lord said to me through this passage: "Don't try to *save* one another. Only God saves." I saw that there was a whole landscape of kindness and promises and daily transactions in which we certainly must trust one another. What would life be if we could not rely on one another's word, did not keep our promises? But then I saw an infinite stretch beyond the far reachings of my soul. I saw that there are needs and longings and hopes and aspirations in me that are somehow infinite. I saw clearly that *for these* I must not trust people. I must not seek in people the ultimate healings and loves that are only possible in God. I saw that sometimes, out of a misguided love and concern, we can try to fill up in another's heart what only God can fill, do for another what only God can do, heal for another what only God can heal.

Where is this line between what I can do for another and what only God can do? I don't know. What I do know is that almost never in the whole of Scripture is the word "trust" used of any other person but God! Maybe this is God's way of telling us that every healing, every love, every happiness that comes to us is ultimately from him. We should not be surprised when we begin to feel the limitations of the human instruments. "I thought she would help, but she didn't." "I counted on him to come through but he didn't." "I thought our relationship would turn out this way and that, but it didn't."

These pains, misunderstandings, disappointments and lack of sensitivities that ebb and flow among us are really part and parcel of the nature of things. They are built-in limitations because *we are limited*. We should say to each other, "Don't trust me for that kind of completeness. Don't be surprised when I don't measure up to all your needs and expectations. Don't trust me for what only God can be and do for you. Please, don't trust me for your salvation!"

I recently came across the following quotation. It expresses something of what I've been trying to say about the inadequacies built into our human relationships. It is God's way of telling us that only *he* can be our everything.

There is a mystery in human hearts, and though we be encircled by a host of people who love us well, and are beloved by us, to every one of us, from time to time, there comes a sense of utter loneliness. Our dearest friend becomes a stranger to our joy and cannot realize our bitterness. We say: 'Nobody really understands me, no one is entering with me into all I feel. I feel so alone.'

Such is the cry of each of us in turn. We wander in a solitary way, no matter what or where our lot may be. Each heart, mysterious even to itself, must live its inner life in solitude.

And would you know the reason this is? It is because the Lord desires our love. In every heart he wishes to be first. He therefore keeps the secret key himself to open all its chambers, and to bless with perfect sympathy and holy peace each solitary soul which comes to him. So when we feel this loneliness it is the voice of Jesus saying: 'Come to me.' And every time we are 'not understood' it is a call to us to come again to Jesus. Only Christ alone can satisfy our hearts. Those who walk with him from day to day can never be on a solitary way.

And when beneath some heavy cross you faint and say 'I cannot bear this load alone,' you speak the truth. Christ purposely made it so heavy that you must turn to him. The bitter grief that comes in the form of 'no one understands,' conveys a secret message from the King, entreating you to come to him again. The Man of Sorrows understands it well. In all points tempted he can feel with you. Only his presence can satisfy the longing soul. Those who walk with him from day to day can never be on a solitary way.

I thought that was really beautiful! Christ certainly wants us to reach out to one another and help one another. But there is a point beyond which we cannot go, and to try to enter that sanctuary is to help create an idol in the heart of another. May the Spirit give us all the discernment to know when we are enticing people to trust us for things we can never be and do for them, and when we are in reality "turning their hearts from Yahweh."

"Come You the Lonely, to the lonely, since You see I am lonely. Come, You who have separated me from everything and made me solitary in this world. Come, my breath and my life. Come, consolation of my poor soul. Come, my joy, my glory, my endless delight'' (St. Symeon).

"I Command You To Love"

One Sunday morning I was reading and praying over the Gospel, when I read the words, "This is my command, that you love one another . . ." I was struck in a new way by the paradox of someone commanding love. If anything goes against our modern sensibilities, surely this does. Certainly love, the free gift of my heart, cannot be commanded.

But as in all other difficult and often mysterious sayings of Jesus, my faith presumption is that *he is right and I don't understand.* I try to remember that I am to be conformed to the Gospel, and not the Gospel conformed to my way of thinking. So I asked the Lord to instruct me especially about these words.

One of the ways he instructed me was by leading me to pray very slowly and meditatively the magnificent 119th Psalm which is all about the commandments of Yahweh as life-giving. I found myself being led by the Lord to take each phrase into my heart, relishing its meaning and making its sentiments my own. How beautiful they are: "Wasting no time, I hurry to your commandments. I stretch out my hands to your beloved commandments, I meditate on your statutes. Teach me good sense and knowledge, for I rely on your commandments. Your commandments epitomize faithfulness. I have noticed limitations to all perfection, but your commandment has no limit at all. I open my mouth, panting eagerly for your commandments. Though distress and anguish grip me, your commandments are my delight.''

It is quite obvious that the author of this psalm, and the myriads of peoples who have prayed this psalm down through the centuries—Jesus himself—saw God's commandments as life-giving and as sure guides on their paths of life.

Maybe this was just an Old Testament notion. Maybe people then had to be commanded because they had a different notion of God and his love for them. But no. Jesus himself often uses the strong word commandment. He talks of the "commandments of God" (Mat. 15:13), about the "first and greatest commandment" (Mk. 12:30); and all during his last discourse the word commandment is frequently on his lips: "This is the command I have been given by my Father" (Jn. 10:18); "No, what I had to speak was commanded by the Father who sent me" (49); "If you keep my commandments you will remain in my love, just as I have kept my Father's commandments and remain in his love" (15:10). Jesus could speak like this because he knew the secret of the Father's commands: "And I know that his commands mean eternal life" (12:50).

We find it difficult to put "command" and "love" together because we have lost our sense of what it is to be a creature. Because we cannot conceive of taking commands from any human authority, we cannot conceive of taking them from God. We instinctively see commands as threats to our freedom. But there are some parallels, even in our human existence, which I think, can show us how commands can be life-giving and not threats.

You are on a passenger ship going across the Atlantic. A terrible storm arises. Orders start booming out over the loudspeaker: "All passengers stay in their cabins. All passengers put on life-preservers." Then finally, "All passengers will proceed to life-boats. We are abandoning ship."

In this situation of extreme danger, and because we believe and trust that the captain knows what he is doing, we follow explicitly his every command. We eagerly wait for the next one. We see his commands at this time as his duty, as our salvation, and we are glad he is giving them and knows what to do. This is a time for commands. We do not expect to hear coming over the loudspeaker something like this: "Attention everyone, that is if you wish to pay attention. Sorry to disturb you. But something has come up. Anyone who would like to—remember this is a request and not a command—but anyone who would like to may now please proceed to the life boats and abandon ship. This is not a command but an invitation. Everyone should feel perfectly free to abandon ship or not. Thank you for your attention."

Well, under such circumstances, people would be very confused. They wouldn't know if the situation was really serious or not. They would argue: "It doesn't sound very serious. We may be all right if we stay on board. I think I'll stay and finish this chess game." No. If the boat is really sinking, the captain must get it across that if the people do not abandon ship, they will drown. If they want to be saved, they are not free to stay on board.

Another example. You are driving out West. You come across a sign, "No Trespassing. Radioactive area. Bomb-testing Site." It's a command you welcome. In fact, if it was not there you would probably sue the government for criminal negligence. The sign is our salvation. Yes, you are "free" to obey the sign or not. But if you want to avoid the danger of radioactivity, you *must* stay out. You are not free to advance if you want to stay out of danger. You are only free to turn around.

The laws of our physical and spiritual nature are much closer to these kinds of commands than they are to invitations. We are "free" to eat or not eat, but if we want to stay alive we are not free to stop eating. You have a (limited) choice about what to eat, but not about eating itself. We are "free" to breathe or not to breathe, but if we want to live we are not free not to breathe. You are free (to a degree) to breathe where you want, but you are not free to stop breathing.

The laws of our spiritual natures work in the same way, though they are less obvious, and there is much more disagreement about them. Man cannot truly live without faith and love. These are the laws of our survival. They are not arbitrary. We are "free" not to believe in God or not to love him, but we are not free if we would truly live. If we would truly live, we *must* believe in and love him.

Our situation is very similar—even much more dangerous and momentous—to that of the sinking ship. Our eternal destiny is at stake. Without the commands of Jesus and his Father we wander aimlessly and frightened on the deck of a sinking ship. It's probably because we do not realize the precariousness of our situation, and because we do not trust God, that we see his commands as threats to our freedom.

Jesus commands us to love because he knows that if we do not love we will die. To love is to abandon the ship of our own selfishness and confusion. If he did not command us, we wouldn't take it too seriously. If we really trusted

him, and realized our own ignorance and need, we too
would see his commands as he saw them, "knowing that
(they) mean eternal life for us."

Chesterton said that "according to Christianity, we were
indeed the survivors of a wreck, the crew of a golden ship
that had gone down before the beginning of the world."
Jesus, as our Lord and God, as our Captain, knows completely the situation we are in. He *commands* us to love.
Yes, we are "free" to love or not, but if we don't love, we
shall die.

Give God a Rest

One weekend it was about 90 degrees in the shade here in
Combermere. The Lord, I think, gave me a word for that
hot summer weekend. I'll attempt to share it with you in
this way.

One of the themes in the Scriptures is about God resting.
In Genesis, the Lord rested after all his work. In Psalm 90
(often prayed before the daily Office) God says: "For for-
ty years I endured that generation and I said, 'They are a
people whose hearts go astray and they do not know my
ways. So, I swore in my anger that they should not enter
my rest.' " And in Psalm 132 we read, "Arise, O Lord,
and go to your resting place, you and the ark of your
might." Then, further on, in verse 13, "For the Lord has
chosen Zion, he has desired it for his habitation: 'This is
my resting place forever; here I will dwell, for I have
desired it.' "

Then there is the reading about the visit of the three
strangers to Abraham, the familiar subject of Rublov's
famous icon of the Trinity. Abraham says to God (in the

person of the three strangers) "My Lord, I beg you—do not pass your servant by. A little water shall be brought; you shall wash your feet and lie down under the tree. Let me fetch a little bread and you shall refresh yourselves before going further"—And they ate while he remained standing near them under the tree.

Then, there is the gospel story of Martha and Mary.

Think of the heat in Palestine during July and August! I've never been there, but I can imagine it goes over a hundred. Jesus, our God, needed a place to relax and refresh himself, a place to rest. Bethany was his place to rest. Throughout the centuries Martha has come in for so much criticism that when we read this story we strain to take her part a little bit and point out how she was simply showing her concern in a different way.

All well and good, but we really shouldn't water down the main point of the story, the point that Jesus was trying to make: He really enjoys just relaxing with us sometimes. With all kinds of people who perhaps don't know him too well, he's busy ministering, teaching, answering questions, healing, consoling, chiding, correcting, etc. Not that he doesn't do this for his close friends also. But with them he looks sometimes for another dimension, another sort of relationship. He simply looks for a place—a heart—where he can come and rest a while from the heat of his labors, from the heat of mankind's sins, from the heat of neglect, from the heat of ingratitude. Jesus is looking for hearts where he can come and be at rest—on vacation, as it were. A heart where he can relax, take off his sandals, and not feel pressured to *do* something for us. He looks for that Bethany space in each of us where he can simply be at home.

We can over-spiritualize here and say that we can have this "Bethany space" no matter what we're doing, that even as we work we can invite the Lord to come and rest in us. This is certainly true. But Jesus could have said the same thing to Martha: She was entertaining the Lord in her own way.

Jesus seems to want something practically different sometimes. He wants us to actually stop working and take time out simply to be with him. He knows we love him in our work. He wants more than our work. He wants us to take time out for him, to relax with him, to simply enjoy his company. We too do not need to say anything, work up some super prayers, plead for all the intentions of the world. There are times for this kind of dialogue. Sometimes, however, Jesus just wants us to relax in his presence and allow him to relax in ours.

Jesus talks about the "one thing necessary" and "the better part." Each one of us will have his or her own understanding of just what that is. But in another passage Saint Paul gives us a clue. He says: "The message which was a mystery hidden for generations and centuries—has now been revealed to his saints. It was God's purpose to reveal it to them and to show all the rich glory of his mystery to the pagans. The mystery is *Christ in you, your hope of glory.*"

The most important thing is to enter constantly more deeply into Jesus who dwells in us. We can do this in a variety of ways. That weekend I heard the Lord saying: "Give me a rest, a vacation in you sometime. Take time out for me and let's just be together, sitting in the shade of a tree, or catching the breezes before an open window. I have so many people coming to me for this, that, and the other thing. I look for people with whom I can relax.''

That weekend was also the feast of Our Lady of Mt. Carmel. Those hermits of the 12th century chose Mary as their model of the perfect contemplative. I like to think that one reason she was chosen was because she knew how to help Jesus relax and rest. I imagine that he often slipped into Nazareth to spend a quiet time with his mother. And I imagine that Mary knew how to protect him from the crowds and from those who needed his ministrations. I imagine that she also tried to arrange places for him elsewhere during his travels, that she would approach him once in a while and say, ''I have secured a little house over in such and such a place. Come and rest a while, relax.'' And then Mary would simply be with him, knowing well how to give him a break from his labors. Mary knew how to relax with Jesus; her heart was the perfect resting place for God.

So, give the Lord Jesus a little vacation in your heart sometimes. There is a monastic phrase—*"vacatio Dei"*—that was used to describe the monks being free for God. ''Being on vacation with God'' is not a bad translation. In our hectic lives let us not forget the Lord's chiding to Martha. Was there really that much work for her to do, or did the Lord sense that there was something else keeping her from relaxing at his feet?

Jesus the Teacher

I took a phone call one night about the death of the step-father of one of our community. As I was walking back to the poustinia, the Lord said to me, ''See how short life is, how precarious. When are you going to do all the things you've been putting off?''

My brothers and sisters, every event in our lives can be seen as an instruction by Jesus. One of the earliest tracts about the Christian life was by Clement of Alexandria (200 A.D.). It was about Jesus the Teacher. Its whole framework was simply that Jesus is the Teacher and we are his children, and that every event of life can be seen as Jesus trying to teach us something about himself.

So when a death occurs, Jesus is teaching us about the brevity of life and asking us when are we going to return his love for us? Or if sadness comes our way, it's Jesus trying to teach us that only God can really fill our hearts, so we should go to him and not put our love in anything or anyone in a way that can never satisfy us.

If it's a joy, we can see it as part of the great joy that he has prepared for us. If we sin, we can see Jesus teaching us how futile is any attempt to seek happiness except in him. And even if everything seems to be going wrong some days—the stew doesn't turn out, we can't get the car started, or whatever—it's Jesus saying to us, "See how really little you can control reality? I'm teaching you about your helplessness, about your lack of ability to do things that you want to do. Depend only on me."

Even if nothing much at all is happening, you can see Jesus teaching you, "Well, wait for me." "As the watchman waits for the dawn, so I wait for you, Lord!" In every moment of our lives, if we are living in faith, we can see an instruction by Our Teacher who is trying to correct us, guide us, encourage us, console us, inspire us, enlighten us—always Jesus.

"Jesus, help us to see you in all the events of our lives. Instruct us about the shortness of life. Teach us about love when we are separated from people. You are always giving us insight into our lives. Lord Jesus, help us always to see you in everything that happens. It is always you, coming to us in some new and life-giving way."

Is Yahweh For Us, or Not?

Exodus tells us that we have all started out in life in the desert, and we were very thirsty. *The desert is not knowing Jesus.* Whatever or whoever else we know, whichever philosophy or ideology we follow, not to know that the Son of God was crucified for us is still to be in the desert.

We started out in this desert not really knowing where we were going or what exactly we were thirsting after, and we carried around inside of us the most nagging of all questions: Is Yahweh for us or against us? Does God exist or not? Does he care about us or not? We wondered if it was ever possible to quench this thirst.

In our desert we challenged God once in a while, like the Hebrew people in the wilderness. We said, "Well, God, *do* something! Make us aware of your presence! Make water come out of a rock or something! Make trees walk around! Show yourself!"

Sometimes God showed himself, and sometimes he didn't. We were still in doubt, still not sure if he was for us or not.

Then one day, as we were busy about our business of filling up water jars (which is our attempt to fill up the well inside us with our buying and selling, our traveling, our studying, our running here and there, doing "new and exciting things"), all of a sudden we heard a voice saying something like this: "You keep drinking that stuff and you'll always be thirsty." Stunned, we stopped and exclaimed, "What?" We heard the voice within us say, "You keep trying to fill up your well with that kind of water and you'll never know what quenching thirst really is."

We stopped dead in our tracks! We began to wonder: Is it possible that Yahweh might be *for* us? Could that be? Is it possible that the thirst that I have can really be quenched? Could that be?

That was our meeting with Christ. He told us about the living waters, and as he spoke we began to experience within us something of what he was talking about. We got all excited. We dropped our water jars, ran here and there, into town and back again, quite beside ourselves. We invited him to stay with us, that is, we asked him to come into our hearts. Yes, we really wanted him to come.

So he came and sat down with us. He did not stay for only a few days, but he stayed with us and remains with us to this very day, teaching us about his Father with his words of everlasting life. That is how our thirst began to be quenched at the fountains of living water, the lips of the Savior.

How happy we should be! There are so many, many people who have never experienced the quenching of their thirst. They are still trying to fill their jars with all kinds of water which we know can never satisfy. How we should long that they too come to these waters! How grateful we should be that God has led us here!

My brothers and sisters, God is thirsty too. On the cross Jesus said, "I thirst." God himself lives in a kind of desert. He lives in the desert of hearts of people who don't seem to know that he is with them and for them. He lives in the desert of hearts, hearts which he wants to fill. But people turn elsewhere, to other wells.

God is really thirsty. God is on a pilgrimage through the world. He is searching for people with great desires so he can fill them. Let us pray for all peoples that they will be filled with immense desires. Let us pray that Jesus will fill them with all his promises, that they will know deep in their hearts that Yahweh is truly for them.

Sons and Daughters of the King

There is a story of an old retired rabbi who used to leave supper early every night. The disciples wondered where he went. The master said, "Oh, he just goes to the synagogue and he stands in prayer, and he delights in God and God delights in him." I think that there are times when God wants us to pray like that. Sometimes even *God* doesn't want to hear about our problems! When Jesus told his disciples to come apart and rest awhile, he didn't explain to them the Last Judgment!

So that's the kind of prayer that we should pray sometime: a prayer of delighting in God and allowing God to delight in us. One of the early great Christian writers, Origen, gave a homily one day, and it was on the Book of Numbers, on the notion of feastdays. Origen was talking about the feastdays of the Jews and of the Christians, and he asked the question, "Does God have any feastdays?" Origen's answer was "Yes. God's feastday is whenever men are being saved. When men are being saved, God has a feastday." Origen quoted the words of the Gospel of Jesus that when a sinner repents, the angels rejoice. Origen reasoned, "Well, if when a sinner repents, angels rejoice, how much more when people love God and when they ac-

cept the Gospel and they share in the mission of Jesus.
What kind of feastday must there not be in heaven with the
angels and the saints?''

We should dwell sometimes on the rejoicing in the hearts
of Jesus and Mary because people are trying to live the
Gospel. We know that their hearts are weighed down with
the sorrows of the world and the rejection of many people
who don't know God, or even hate him. But the hearts of
Our Lady and of Jesus also rejoice and feast with us. They
are delighting in what is happening in our hearts. And why
are they rejoicing? Because the plan of God is being fulfilled in us—the plan that all men should walk in love in his
presence. They rejoice that the prayer of Jesus that
laborers come into the harvest is being fulfilled in us. They
rejoice because we, in our poor way, are saying ''Yes,
Amen—So be it—Lord I want to share in your plan for the
world. Be it done unto me according to your word.''

My brothers and sisters, was there ever a vision of life
such as the vision that we have? That we are created to
walk in love. That Jesus calls us, teaches us, gives us his
Spirit of love to bless and heal and to teach men about the
love of his Father! He invites us to share in this great work.
Was there ever a vision of life, was there ever a vocation
like our vocation? We think that *we* are searching for God.
The first words of God after man's sin were, ''Man, where
are *you?*'' God is searching for us much more that we are
searching for him. The Bible is about God coming after us,
seeking us, longing for us, thirsting for us. Every day there
is a great feast in heaven because some people have said yes
to this longing of God for our love.

Very simply, that's the spirit, that's the message I have
to share with you. Let us delight in the Lord and let the

Lord delight in us. During our lives we will have many difficulties and problems and struggles. The Fathers say there is only one real temptation; that it is *to forget that we are sons and daughters of the King.* The only real temptation is to forget that we are loved by God, not to remember that Jesus died for us out of love. That is the basic fact and vocation of our lives, to be loved by God. The only infallible prayer, Thomas Merton says, is to pray to be loved by God. Let us never forget that we are all sons and daughters of the King.

Holy Families

The feast of the Holy Family is very dear to us at Madonna House. The spirit of Nazareth and of a family of love are very much at the heart of our way of life. I would just like to share briefly a few quotations from Catherine's writings on the theme of Nazareth and the Holy Family. These are not just haphazard quotations, but they come from very significant sources and from very significant times in her life.

The first is from the *History of Our Apostolate.* In the very opening pages she writes this: "Nazareth for me meant a novitiate with Our Lord, Our Lady and St. Joseph, a school of love to which I had to go if I were to do what my heart seemingly wanted so much to do—namely, restore the whole world to Christ."

In 1965, Catherine went into poustinia to try to clarify for herself what the essence of our vocation was. She wrote several lines which for her summed up our way of life: "The spirit of Madonna House is living and preaching the Gospel with your life, and through this, forming a com-

munity of love, a family, a community of love that brings
Love's love to individuals. And Madonna House spirit
takes its strength and example from Bethlehem, Nazareth
and the kenosis of Golgotha. I have been thinking much
lately about our vocation and it seems to me that it is
Nazareth, a hidden little village to which we have to go and
live with the Holy Family to become whole again.''

My brothers and sisters, this mystery of Nazareth is very
profound. There is a cycle of evil in the world, and a great
deal of it is perpetuated in our families. We grow up into a
family. Our parents are imperfect, and our brothers and
sisters are imperfect. Before we have learned to love one
another, we leave our home, sometimes forced out by our
brothers and sisters or our families, the pressure of our
culture. Then we go out and start our own families before
we are healed. We perpetuate the evils and the problems of
our parents, and their parents, and their parents.

What is Jesus' solution to this problem? Well, very
simply, it's to believe that we can grow to love the people
with whom we live. Jesus stayed home. For thirty years he
lived in one place with certain people. He won for all of us
the grace to make *any* home, a real home. He showed us
that it is possible to love the people with whom we live. We
do not have to run away. We do not have to keep traveling,
to keep moving. The mystery of Nazareth is that Jesus has
won what seems to us the almost impossible grace: to love
the people with whom we live, our parents and our
brothers and sisters, our husbands, wives, and children.

Isn't that, after all, one of the hardest things? Isn't that
what we are nervous about? Don't we really believe, deep
down, that we will ever be able to love our own family?
Think of your own family. Wouldn't you desire most of all

that you could be one with your parents, with your brothers and sisters? It's possible! Jesus lived it to make that grace available to us.

The Kingdom Is Here

You'll be happy to know that there's one thing that all the scripture scholars agree on, that is, that *the* theme, the central aspect of the teaching of Jesus was the kingdom of God. Everybody agrees. It's the theme that runs through most of Our Lord's parables, the thread that ties them together: the banquet, and the seed falling into the ground represent the kingdom of God. In the consciousness of Christ, in his person and in his teachings, he said that the kingdom of God is here, present among us. For this he gave his life.

What is the kingdom of God? A kingdom is whatever one rules over. And what does God want to rule over most? *Our hearts.* There is nothing else worth ruling. The kingdom of God is God's power and feast and joy already at work in our hearts—building them into a kingdom worthy of himself. Jesus said that this kingdom is happening, it's here. For anybody who wants to know what true peace is, true joy, the truth—it's available here for the taking.

People talk today about revolutions, and even Christian revolution. My brothers and sisters, the most revolutionary thing we can do is to be witnesses to the kingdom that is present among us. It is an explosive reality. We all know that it's much easier to keep busy rather than simply to allow his kingdom to come in our own hearts. If anybody wants to be a true revolutionary in the world, all he has to do is let the kingdom come within him. Then God will use him beyond his wildest dreams. The kingdom of God is here. Probably one of the saddest things we can do is to doubt that that is true.

We have a lot of different faults, you and I. One of the faults that militates most against what Jesus came to do is to believe that the kingdom is not here. To believe that sadness is deeper than joy, to believe that the evils in the world are more powerful than God.

Let us ask for great faith in the presence of the kingdom. Let's pray that by our poverty, our life of love, whatever the Holy Spirit wants to do in our lives, we witness to what everybody is looking for. They want to know if the kingdom is really happening. They want to know if there really is any peace or any joy or truth in our hearts. We say, "Yes, there is. And it's starting to grow already." Let us pray for great faith in the kingdom growing already in our hearts. Let's not be afraid to tell other people about it. Because that's what they're looking for. They want to know if God is alive, if he has done anything for us. We say, "Yes, a thousand times, yes."

The Greatest Armada In History

It is sometimes said that the Armada that was assembled to attack the beach of Normandy in the Second World War was the greatest attack force in history. There were something like 60,000 different kinds of boats crossing the Channel. People say that was the greatest assault in the history of the world. It's not true.

The greatest assault, the greatest attack, in the history of the world was Jesus riding into Jerusalem. Christ was fighting the battle of all battles. He was attacking the root of all evil. He attacked the root of man's hardness of heart and he fought against death itself. Jesus riding into Jerusalem was the greatest Armada on earth.

Because Christ was God, we often play down the fact that Jesus *freely chose* what he was doing. There were other times in his life when he avoided his enemies. He said it wasn't time, it wasn't "my Father's time."

When things came to a head in his struggle with the Pharisees, Christ could have chosen a number of things. He could have chosen to leave the country. The tension was building up. He could have just written those people off his list. No sense trying to reach them. Or, Jesus could have simply gone back to Nazareth and given up the whole thing. He could have organized some kind of political revolution. (It seems from the Gospel that he had an awful lot of popular support.)

But Jesus knew very well what the main issue was all about. With full insight and full knowledge and full freedom, he rode defenseless into Jerusalem and gave himself into the hands of his enemies. We say that *by that act we are saved.* Jesus knew that there was no other way to overcome the hardness of our hearts, except to ride into Jerusalem that day. And he chose it freely.

He knew that there was *no other way of showing them that God is more powerful than anything that they could do.* That God was more powerful than death itself. By this act he revealed to us the power of God his Father. He revealed to us the power of love. He revealed to us the mystery that is at work in the heart of the world.

Part of our joy, our great joy, should be that, by our faith, we know what the mystery of life is all about: It's life through death. Jesus never said it was going to be easy. But he said it was the truth, and that he would be with us.

He revealed to us how to overcome sin in our lives. He revealed to us how to overcome evil in the hearts of others. He revealed to us the other side of death. And what a great joy it should be, that in faith, we know that this is true. We can only rejoice because Jesus freely chose to ride into Jerusalem that day.

The best way that we can thank Christ is by living out this mystery in our own lives. Every time we choose another way except love, we do something of what Judas did. We say: "Jesus, your way is not the best way and it won't work, ever." For each one of us, at some point in our journey to Easter, suffering love, the defenseless ride to Jerusalem, will be the only way. Let us pray for each other that we will come to a deeper understanding then of the mystery of paschal life through death. It's not easy, but it's the only way. If there were another way, Jesus would have told us and he would have taken it himself.

Because he went before us, we can do it too. We can walk behind him to Jerusalem. We can love when love doesn't make any sense. We can hope when there's no reason to hope. We can do all these things in the strength of him who loved us freely, and who saved us by launching his victorious attack that day in Jerusalem.

By His Rejection We Are Healed

Jesus died of a broken heart. Somehow he experienced a total rejection so that we might experience a total acceptance.

People involved in the healing ministry in the charismatic renewal tell us that at least one person in five has to be healed of some kind of rejection in his or her past. They've discovered, for example, that some people born during the Depression learned that they were really not wanted at the time because of the scarcity of food and money. Sometimes children are simply not wanted by their mothers. Each of us, in his or her own way, experienced rejection of some kind, either from our peer groups or from our families. What is it to be rejected? It's the experience of not being wanted, being on the outside, not belonging.

I ask you to look into your own hearts for a few moments and perhaps think of those rejections, large or small as they are, and to understand that Jesus experienced rejection at a very profound level. Somehow he even experienced rejection by his Father as he cried out on the cross. That means that there is no kind of rejection that you can ever experience that Jesus has not gone through and conquered and transformed. However dark it may seem, Jesus is present there, and if you can believe in him, that he is present there, you will be able to see in your own heart acceptance and victory and love.

He went through all those things to show us that he is stronger than death, stronger than any kind of rejection that we'll ever have to bear. He died of a broken heart for you so that you might never be crushed by rejection again.

Out of the Sacred Heart of Jesus that was broken open for you pours all the healing that you need for whatever rejection you've had or ever will have to face. "Jesus, we know that we will never have to face the rejection that you have allowed yourself to feel. Your heart was so sensitive. You knew what it was, somehow, to even be abandoned by the Father. Lord, we take our rejections now, the little ones, the big ones, and place them in your heart, and we know that you are present with us there, and we believe in you, and we see you victorious over all those hurts in our lives. And we thank you Jesus for suffering rejection for us and other people, for those who are dear to us. We praise you for entering those dark areas of life so that we can always be with you, no matter where we find ourselves. Lord Jesus, may the grace of your Sacred Heart wash us. May we all experience the total acceptance that you want for us. And we thank you for your love and your mercy in our lives. Lord have mercy.''

I Will Go Where You Go

There is something exquisitely beautiful about Ruth's attitude towards Naomi. For these words strike our hearts: "Wherever you go, Naomi, I will go too; and whoever your people are, they will be my people; and whatever God you worship will be my God.'' Ruth's love for Naomi somehow is greater than her dedication to her own people and even for the gods that she serves.

Ruth's dedication is a beautiful definition of faith. It is what our relation to Jesus should be. We do not try to work out a theory of God and then see if Jesus agrees with it. We do not try to work out a theory of faith and then see if Jesus can help us with it. The very center of our life is this following of *Jesus* which illuminates everything else.

Faith is really saying to Jesus, "I don't know who God is, but whatever God you serve, I want to serve him. Jesus, I don't know what the future holds, but Jesus, wherever you go, wherever you lead me, I want to go with you." This love, this personal love for Jesus, is the key—the key to faith, the key to the future, the key to everything. Like

Ruth, we say to Jesus, "Wherever you go, that's where I'm going."

Not only do we belong to Jesus, but Jesus belongs to us. Jesus, his heart, his desires, his wishes, his hopes, his dreams and his love for the Father. Everything is ours. Jesus belongs to us. And what is Jesus trying to do most of all but give us this passionate love for himself? We don't have to work out theological problems. All we have to do is fall in love with Jesus and the Father.

"Jesus, wherever you go, we will go. Your people will be our people, your God will be our God, your desires will be our desires, your hopes will be our hopes, your loves will be our loves. Jesus, give us a passionate love for you, to follow wherever you go. Draw us after you."

Joy Also Redeems

Sometimes when we pray we have what we call distractions. Some of them really are distractions and we have to get rid of them. But sometimes the things we call distractions are possibly things the Lord might want us to pray about, situations in our lives, or people. We can turn them into prayers.

One weekend the community was preparing for a Variety Show. I'm sure it was the cause of "distractions" for many people during their prayers and liturgies. Well, the same thing happened to me: As I was preparing the readings one night I couldn't stop thinking about the Variety Show. And the Lord said: "Well, why don't you consider *my presence* in the Variety Show? Remember, joy also redeems."

We don't have any problems with seeing our penances,

or the crosses that come along, as somehow helping Jesus
save the world. We give them to Christ and he uses them.
But Jesus said to me, "Tell them that when they're having
a good time and really rejoicing in my presence, tell them
that this joy is also going out and redeeming the world."

If you don't believe that, my brothers and sisters, you
have a really strange idea of who God is and what he's all
about. Because it's not really suffering *or* joy that gives
life, but *love*. Suffering without love, or joy without love,
are both useless, as St. Paul taught us. Joy is not a
"break" from our way of life, but joy too is redemptive.

When Jesus in the Gospel went to Zaccheus' house and
had a good time, he was also saving us. And Mary says,
"My soul magnifies the Lord, and my spirit rejoices."
When Mary rejoiced, her joy also was part of Jesus' saving
action.

Love redeems. Love-filled joy is part of God's plan, for
that too will be put into the hands of Christ and will help to
save the world. It would follow then that the more joyful
we are, the better it will be for everybody!

God's Longing for Us

Don't put too much emphasis on *your* longing for God.
Think of God longing for *you*. Because God's desires for
us are so much more than our desire for him.

Imagine the longing of Jesus for you. "With longing
have I longed to eat this meal with you," Jesus said. What
must be the longing of God to come into our lives! If we
put the emphasis here, it gives us great hope. We'll not be
afraid because we'll see that our wanting God is not
presumptuous. It's not our program but it's God's plan for

us. That is our hope and that is our joy. God desires us beyond our wildest imagination.

Secondly, remember that if you're longing for God to come into your life, try and be aware of what you're seeking. You're asking for the *living God to come*. You don't know exactly what that will mean. You're not longing for some kind of spiritual high. You're not asking for God to come and confirm your own illusions about yourselves or about him. You're asking for God himself.

If you pray "Come Lord Jesus," you're asking God to come and shake the foundations of your life. That's okay, because they have to be shaken. God has to reveal ourselves to ourselves. But in your prayer, when you pray "Come Lord Jesus," remember what you're asking for. God wants to come; he'll be with you. But he might turn your life upside down. He might change your attitudes; in fact, he will! So be aware of what you're asking. You're asking the living God to invade your life.

God is much more interested in the future than in the past. We think of God often as conserving things. But what God has in store for us is so much greater than what has already happened. So if you feel yourself in any way looking backwards instead of forwards, you may be losing some of your spiritual childhood and some of your spiritual youth. Jesus wants us to look ahead. He has great things for us to do. He has great graces to pour into our hearts.

When we love someone we stand on tiptoes and say, "Where is she?" or "When is he coming?" There is also a longing in us to see God. When God comes, he does not come by bits and pieces; the whole Christ comes to us. In every Eucharist the entire Christ comes to us. It's only our lack of faith that prevents us from being totally open to him.

The Final Stage of Wisdom

In John's Gospel (12, 20-33) we witness the only time when Jesus speaks to the Greeks. Like the other Gospel stories, it's a shame we don't have more of the conversation. I would like to give you a little background of this encounter between Jesus and the Greeks in this Gospel.

For hundreds of years before Christ came, men were intensely involved in the search for truth and wisdom. It was the time when the Jews themselves wrote their Wisdom literature—the Book of Proverbs, Job, and Ecclesiastes. In Israel, wisdom took on a religious form—wisdom comes from God, and wisdom is keeping God's law.

Outside of Israel, wisdom took a different turn. Among the Greeks, wisdom took the form of philosophy, and the Greeks became the humanists of their day. They were supposed to have a kind of "market" on wisdom and truth. It's to their credit that they sought out Jesus. They came, and they wanted to see him and talk with him. The conversation must have been very interesting, because the way the Greeks went about looking for truth was quite different from the way the Hebrews, the people of the East, did.

The Gospel says the Greeks came to *see* Jesus, and that's the way they looked for truth. They put the truth out in front of them and they sat and looked at it and analyzed it and tore it apart with their minds. For them, if they could *see* clearly, they had the truth in their heads.

But for the Hebrews, truth is much more a matter of the heart. For the Hebrew, the truth is a passionate involvement with reality. That's why the psalmist says, "Lord, give me a pure *heart,"* not a clear mind.

We could imagine that Jesus and these Greeks were talking on different levels. The Greeks were perhaps looking for a very elaborate explanation of what wisdom really is. But Jesus said to them, "Unless the seed falls into the ground and dies, it remains alone." He said to them: "Do you want to know what wisdom is? Follow me. Do what I do."

Now we don't know what happened to these men. They might have become intense followers of Christ. But Jesus was saying that the whole end of the wisdom movement was an involvement with God. And not only that, but if you become involved with God, you're going to come up against suffering. When that happens, don't try and understand it with your head and figure out what is wrong. Jesus comes to reveal to us the final stage of wisdom, and it is a hard saying. The final stage of wisdom is that if you love enough, you are going to suffer. But in that involvement you will understand who God is and you will come to the deepest understanding of life that is possible.

The Greeks looked for wisdom; in many ways we are still like them. Because when we come up against the cross we start to ask all kinds of questions: "What is going wrong? Something is not right with my 'self-development.' Things don't seem to be working out the way they should be." The cross for us is still a scandal. We don't mind the cross as long as we can get on top of it and handle it. But the cross that we can't get on top of and that wipes out all our feelings and emotions of how things ought to run, that kind of cross is still a scandal to us. Jesus says that the final stage of wisdom is to suffer in love and to *see with one's heart* that God is there. Unless Christ had done that, nobody would have believed it, and the search for wisdom would still be going on.

Jesus prayed to his Father to deliver him from death. Jesus still died, but the scriptures say that his prayer was answered. He was given by his Father the faith and the love and the courage to move into death and to overcome it and to reveal to us the secret of wisdom that is found in suffering love.

Don't misunderstand! Some people think that the drive within us is towards suffering. No, the drive in us is towards loving. The convenant relationship that we have in our hearts is towards greater and greater love. But the life of Christ says to us: If you love deeply enough and constantly, you will meet suffering. When that happens, don't stop there and think that the world is falling apart. You have to keep going. That's the scandal. That's what we need strength for.

As we suffer, we become more sensitive. As we become more sensitive, we are able to hear God's word better. As we hear God's word better, we respond more and we suffer more and then we become more sensitive. There is no end to this cycle, and Jesus says, "Don't stop. Keep going. On the other side of death is the resurrection."

We rejoice in the presence of Christ. He died for us and revealed the final stage of God's wisdom. We believe in the Covenant, which means that God is our friend. If God is our *friend,* then what will we fear? If, like for Jesus, God is our friend, our Father, then God is strong enough to deliver us from every suffering that we encounter on our journey. He is strong enough to deliver us from death itself.

And so, while we rejoice in the presence of Jesus, let us pray for this gift of true wisdom, that when we love, and suffering happens to us, we will not stop, but we will follow Jesus who had joy placed before him and suffered everything for our sake.

"Woe to you, scribes and Pharisees, hypocrites"
(Matt. 23, 27).

Thank goodness such passages do not apply to us! (Now you probably think that this opening sentence is being used for dramatic effect, and that my very next sentence will be, "But of course it applies to us!") No. I really mean what I say: it doesn't apply to us—at least I know it doesn't apply to me! Jesus is not talking to me here. He's talking to a group of really hard-hearted people who completely rejected him.

It's important when we read the Scriptures to remember that each of us has a relationship to a living and present Jesus, not the Jesus who spoke the passages in the gospels. Oh, it's the same Jesus. But he spoke those words two thousand years ago to certain people in certain circumstances. One of the keys for understanding the gospels is to see all the words of Jesus as coming from a personal relationship with Jesus. In my relationship with Jesus, I cannot imagine him saying to me, "Woe to you, Robert Wild." Jesus doesn't talk to me that way. For many years I've been trying to love him, trying to serve his people, trying to live the Gospel. I have a deep sadness always because I do not do this very well. But I'm trying, and I believe Jesus appreciates my efforts.

So when I read this passage, I hear something like this:

"I have given you many gifts and opportunities. You have responded to some of them but you know as well as I that many opportunities you have let slip by. If I had given the same gifts to some other people I think some of them would have been more generous than you."

I do not relate to the Jesus of two thousand years ago. He is for me a living Person, and my relationship with him has certain dimensions and characteristics. That is why each passage of Scripture should mean something slightly different for each of us, because our relations with Jesus are slightly different. We should never hear any of these words in a way that makes Jesus inhuman or unreal. He may speak harsh words sometimes; we all need that. But if we hear our best Friend saying "Woe is you," then I think we are not considering deeply enough our own personal relationship. We are merely lifting words out of a text and disregarding the living presence of our Friend.

"Show Us the Spirit And It Will Be Enough For Us"

There is really only one mystery of life: It is the Word of God who is trying to bring everything to completion as God planned it. There are many things in creation that just naturally come to completion: flowers grow, all the fruits of the field ripen. But this mystery in man has a special problem, because of man's sin. When we speak of the mystery of life in us, we speak of the *Paschal mystery*. Man has to cross the Red Seas and Jordan Rivers to get where God has promised to meet him. In our own lives too we have to cross the Red Sea and the desert places. We say that Jesus is the one who leads us. Jesus is the mystery in

us. He has revealed to us how to live and how to return to
the Father. He has done this by his life, his death, his
resurrection, his ascension, and by the sending of the
Spirit. Jesus is now at the Father's right hand forever. He
has shown us how to live; he has shown us how to die; and
now at the Father's right hand he sends his Spirit and he
puts fire into all the words he has spoken to us, into all the
deeds he has lived, into all the sufferings he has endured.
Jesus is eternally now at the Father's right hand and he is
sending his spirit on all of creation, to all parts of the
earth, to complete the mystery of life in us, to bring us
back to the Father.

One day the disciples said, "Lord, just show us the
Father and that will be enough for us." (He had been talking about the Father.) Jesus replied: "Don't you understand yet? When you see me, you see the Father!" I think
that sometimes we do exactly the same thing with the Holy
Spirit. "But Lord, you've been talking about the Holy
Spirit; just show him to us and that will be enough." I hear
Jesus saying to us, "How can you say, 'Show us the Holy
Spirit?' Don't you believe that the peace that you ex-
perience in your lives right now is the Holy Spirit in you to-
day? And the love that you have for one another is not a
natural love. Don't you believe that that is the Holy Spirit?
How can you say, 'Lord, just show me the Holy Spirit?'
You are able to pronounce my name; you can say, 'Jesus is
Lord.' No one can say that Jesus is Lord without the Holy
Spirit. How can you say, 'Lord, show us the Holy Spirit!'
The reverence that you have for my Father, this is inspired
by my Holy Spirit. How can you say, 'Lord, just show us
the Spirit!' Don't you believe that it is my Spirit that is in-

spiring you to pray to my Father?'' The Holy Spirit is so close to us, he is so near to us, in all these faith actions that are part of our lives.

At Pentecost we celebrate the birth of the Church. The apostles and early followers of Jesus were separated from one another, isolated, just a group of people. On this day, Jesus, at the right hand of the Father, sent his Holy Spirit upon them and wove them not only into one body but into one soul, one living organism, and they became his Church. From that creation they could go forth and talk about Jesus as they never talked about him before.

Do you feel separated from anyone? Do you feel disunited? Today and every day that same power is available to you. Jesus wants to unite us and send the Holy Spirit and break down whatever divisions are among us. He wants to create this one soul, this one living organism.

Saint Paul talks about the gifts of the Holy Spirit. Jesus knew that we could not save ourselves and could not love him and others without special help. So he says to us today and every day of our lives, ''What do you need? Do you need healing in some area of your life? Ask for it and I will send my Holy Spirit. Do you feel alone and separated from others? I don't want you to be orphans. Ask for my Holy Spirit. He will come and dissolve your loneliness. Do you feel you cannot speak a word about my Father? Ask, and I will send my Holy Spirit and you will be able to speak words of God.''

Anything that we need to get back to the Father, Jesus has won for us by his death and rising. He has given us his Holy Spirit; his own love and knowledge he has poured into our hearts. His very own love, his very own joy, his very own courage, his very own *self,* his very own everything.

Jesus has not just given us a few gifts, he has given us *the* gift—the Holy Spirit.

Jesus knows that our sins burden us and so the Holy Spirit within us testifies to the resurrected Christ, that Jesus has *conquered* sin and death. Do you have sins that are burdens? "I give you power," Jesus says in the Gospel, "to forgive sins, to mediate forgiveness to others by my Holy Spirit." This mystery of the Spirit coming is continuous in our own lives: Jesus pouring him out through the wounds that he shows to his Father forever and ever.

Recently one of the members of our family died. We all shared what the Holy Spirit was saying to us about his death and its meaning for our community. One of the answers that came to me was this: Did you ever notice how great people become after their death! Death takes the scales from our eyes and we see people in the deepest part of their hearts. And that is what happened with Paul. Paul was among us for many, many years, and we saw this and that about him; but when death came we tried to see him with the deeper eyes of faith, and what beautiful things we saw about Paul! They were always present, but somehow when death comes the Holy Spirit opens our eyes and we see people as they really are. This *actually* happened with Jesus. When Jesus walked among his disciples and friends, how could they see, how could they know who he was? But when Jesus died, the Holy Spirit came and revealed to them Jesus' deepest identity.

I think that one of the gifts of the Holy Spirit is the gift of seeing each other as we really are in God's eyes. If we could only have a little of that vision that we get after someone dies! Imagine if you had died yesterday and you could hear people talking about you. You might not even

recognize yourself! All the things that people are saying!
Wow! But it is true, it is true! Maybe death is what we have
to pay for the strength to believe in ourselves. We can't
believe that God has done such wonderful things to each of
us. That is why we find it hard to say them to each other.
So one of the gifts I think the Spirit wants to give us is that
we see each other much more profoundly than ever before.
Something of how we will see and think about each other
after death.

"Who Can Resist the Day of the Lord?" (I Can!)

During my poustinia days one week the story of the rich
man and Lazarus (Luke 16,19) had been popping in and
out of my mind. The "word" which gradually took form
in my heart this week was "courage," courage to face the
truth of my present situation before God. I discovered in
the Lazarus story several hard truths—"hard
sayings"—which helped to clarify for me my present situation.

Origen (I think) said that only the Christian really
understands what sin is, because only the Christian
understands to what lengths God has gone to win our love
in Christ. It is a real grace from God to be able to confront
our sins; a grace too to be able to look at hard truths head
on without being overwhelmed or depressed by them. If we
cannot face our sins squarely, we will never know what a
Savior is. If we cannot admit our present procrastinations,
we will not experience the power of God's Word, calling us
to greater efforts.

God's Word is very powerful—especially when we apply

it to ourselves! The "hard sayings" contained in the Lazarus story have the power to transform our lives if we can only have the courage to "let them into our awareness" and confront us where we are at the present moment.

The rich man is blithely enjoying himself. He doesn't come across to us as a particularly evil person. (Even in his pain he has a thought for his relatives.) But he is living quite blind to proper values. He is living in a dream world. To some extent, we are like him. Everything depends on our facing this truth: that there are some areas of our lives which are false, where we are blinded to real values, living in a dream world. The particular maliciousness of the rich man's situation or frame of mind is that he didn't seem to be overly concerned about discovering truth and justice.

Death came quickly, and it will come quickly for us too. My brothers and sisters, how much more time do we really have—20, 30, 40 years? Fleeting moments! Perhaps the rich man thought of helping Lazarus—but tomorrow, or next week. What's the rush? He's been there so long, he'll be there tomorrow. So we too keep putting off what we know God is asking of us. The days flow into weeks, the weeks into months, the months into years. There's time! Take it easy!

It is part of the story too that some people do not change. The rich man resisted God right up to his dying day. Awesome and frightful power! In one of the prophets it says, "Who can resist the day of the Lord?" I remember saying, "I can!" It's in our power to resist, to stay right where we are. The story goes on to relate that there is some kind of punishment for such conscious resistance.

For me, the most striking lines come in the last two answers of Abraham. The rich man pleads that something *more* be done so that his brothers do not fall into the same predicament. Abraham replies that for people whose hearts are in the right place and who have eyes to see, enough has been done, enough has been given.

How true this is for the Christian! How much we have been given! What possible excuse will we use when we come before the Lord! What advantage didn't we enjoy? What helps and mutual assistance did we not have access to? What opportunities to grow in love were lacking to us? "They have Moses and the Prophets, Jesus and the Church, let them listen to them."

And then comes what for me is the most powerful line in the whole story: ". . . they will not be convinced even if someone should rise from the dead."

I began listing my own lines of resistance, the areas of my life where I have taken a stand against the onslaught of God's grace. And in each of these areas I have tried to allow the voice of Christ to confront me: "You will not overcome those fears even if I should rise from the dead. You will not enter more deeply into prayer even if I should rise from the dead. You will not try to get closer to this or that person even if I should rise from the dead."

Jesus does not tell us such stories because he likes to scare people. He tells us such stories because he loves us. Life *is* serious. Our choices *are* for keeps. Once in a while perhaps we need to be scared into realizing that conscious resistance to grace is part of our lives. We need to reflect that time is short, and that we do not have many valid excuses for not growing in love.

They cannot scare me with their empty spaces
Between stars—on stars where no human race is.
I have it in me so much nearer home
To scare myself with my own desert places.

Robert Frost

"If an Enemy Were Making Fun of Me, I Could Endure It"
(Ps.35,12)

I spent one Lent with the prophet Jeremiah. Not a very cheery prophet, for the most part. His mission was to "tell it like it is" to a people who had gone very far off the path of goodness:

Yahweh says this:
I remember the affliction of your youth,
the love of your bridal days:
you followed me through the wilderness,
through a land unsown,
Israel was sacred to Yahweh,
the first fruits of his harvest—(2, 1-3)

Take careful notice and observe
if anything like this has happened.
Does a nation change its gods?
. . . .
Yet my people have exchanged their Glory
for what has no power at all.
You heavens, stand aghast at this,
stand stupefied, and utterly appalled,
. . . . my people have committed a double crime:

they have abandoned me,
the fountain of living water,
only to dig cisterns for themselves,
leaky cisterns that hold no water (10-13).

If a man divorces his wife
and she leaves him
to marry someone else,
may she still go back to him?
Has not that piece of land
been totally polluted?
And you, who have prostituted yourself with so many
     lovers,
you would come back to me (3,1)

..............my people are stupid,
they do not know me,
they are slow-witted children,
they have no understanding:
they are clever enough at doing wrong,
but do not know how to do right (4,22).

Admittedly, my brothers and sisters, these are harsh words. But Lent is the time for such words. The Church, in the wisdom of the liturgical year, knows how to emphasize now one aspect of our life with God, now another. At Easter we will rejoice and sing, hardly remembering our backslidings and our failings. During Advent we yearn for the Lord in hope, not looking so much on our sins as on the Lord's promise to save us in spite of them. During much of the year we listen at the feet of Christ to his teachings, weighing his words in our hearts and looking for direction and meaning.

And Lent? Lent is a time for looking squarely at our sins. To be sure, never without remembering Easter and Christmas and the Spirit within us, but for all that, admitting into our hearts a sharper focus upon those acts by which we deliberately and consciously refuse to follow God's inspirations within us.

"But," we are tempted to say, "those words of Jeremiah are a bit much. Rather over-dramatic! Using all sorts of powerful images mostly for effect! Prostituting myself with other lovers! Changing my God for other gods! Clever at doing wrong! Excuse me, but in all honesty, I'm really not that bad!"

My brothers and sisters, as I read these words of Jeremiah that Lent I tried to discipline myself to think of nobody else. Not to apply them to Israel, to Watergate, to Hitler, to the kidnappers of Patricia Hearst—to no one but *myself*. I'd like to share with you what the Lord taught me.

If I compare my life and actions with Hitler, with a civilization at its worst, or with the leaders of international dope rings, then (by the grace of God) I'm not doing too badly! Because the words are so powerful ("prostituted yourself with so many lovers") and because I can't see myself as "all that bad," the temptation is either to apply them to somebody else, or at least to minimize them a bit in regard to myself!

The Lord taught me that the quality, depth, and seriousness of acts depends not so much on acts "in themselves" but on the context of the relationship in which they take place. We know there is a difference, say, between two guys in school punching one another in the hall between classes, a husband slapping his wife (whom he doesn't love very much anyway) and a Christian slapping another in the face out of real malice and anger. They are all the same actions, but somehow one is more serious than the others, because the context is different; *in the last case it comes from a person who has been given so much by Christ and has been the recipient of so much of his love.*

I think you see what I am getting at. We are not to compare our failings with those of Hitler, or the kidnappers, or the international Mafia. We ought to evaluate all our refusals in the light of everything God has done for *us. Very few people have received so much love and consolation and light as we have.* As Christians, we know and realize to some extent that Jesus died for us and that now, in some mysterious way, he depends on us for the furthering of his kingdom. Every day we are invited to the Eucharist, to the Scriptures, to share in a thousand and one supports in our life with Christ. Our refusals should be seen *in this light—in the light of the overwhelming love that Christ has shown to us.*

If Jesus were more real to us we would experience that our refusals are indeed prostitutions, stupidities, extremely clever ways of doing wrong. If all our acts were evaluated in the light of our own personal relationship to Jesus, the words of Jeremiah would not seem all that extravagant!

How can we stand up under such devastating words? We can, *because the words of consolation are ours too.* There are occasions, however, for soul-searching, for letting our failures sear a bit into our consciousness. Strange prayer, but my prayer is that we will not be afraid to face squarely our sins, and this, not in comparison with Watergate or anyone else, but in the light of what Jesus has done for *us*. "To whom much has been given, much will be required."

The Magnificence of Forgiveness

Life together is a matter of how much courage we have to be able to preach the Gospel specifically to one another.

Jesus said that if our lives are built on him, on the Rock that is, on his word, nothing will be able to shake us—nothing. But if our lives are not built on the Gospel, there will be weaknesses and cracks where all kinds of influences and spirits can come in.

The world is like a disaster situation because of sin. And when we are in disaster situations, we do not calculate our responses to peoples' needs. When people are in a situation of real peril, we do not calculate how much to give them. Our hearts say, "Sure!" and we don't make a mental reservation, "Well, in the next disaster, they'll have to help me." There is something about a crisis situation: We just open our hearts and say, "Yes. Take it. Here. I don't care. What does it matter!"

The call to us all our lives is the call to forgiveness. It is a call to stop weighing the past, to stop drawing up lists; it is a call to enter as deeply as we can into the magnificent, the most divine quality that Christ has given us: the quality of forgiveness.

I don't know if there is anything that we can do that is closer to God than to forgive. People can go and work in the slums, and that is a beautiful thing; people can go into the desert and have glorious experiences of God, great insights; and that is a beautiful thing too. But I really don't believe there is anything more sublime or closer to the heart of God than to forgive one another. One of the last things that Jesus said to us on the Cross was, "Father, forgive them. . . ."

Did you ever stop to think that God is the only person who really doesn't have to forgive? Jesus: he is the only person who really hasn't sinned or done anything against us. He is the only person who by right, when you think about it, would not have to forgive. He hasn't done anything wrong. And he is the one who forgives most of all. He is the one who has taken on himself all our lack of forgiveness, all of our sins. He has become sin. He hung on the cross and he said, "Father, forgive them."

When we hear Jesus saying "Love your enemies," one of our first reactions is: "He must be kidding! Love your enemies? Whom is he talking to?" Jesus responds, "I'm talking to *you.*" We protest: "Lord, you don't know who *I* am." He answers, "Yes, I do. I know who you are better than *you* do. *You* don't know who you are. You don't know what greatness is in your heart. You don't know the reaches that your spirit is able to attain. *You* don't know who you are. But *I* know. And I am calling you to greatness: Love your enemies!"

What a magnificent picture of man Jesus has! There are all sorts of images of man: man as a machine, man as an animal. Jesus says, "I am the only one who knows what man really is. And I say that man is able to forgive his enemies. He is able, when someone slaps him, to turn the other cheek." You, my brothers and sisters, can do it too. If you say you can't, you don't know who you are. You don't know who Jesus is calling you to be. If someone forces us to walk where we don't want to walk, Jesus says

we *can* walk farther. If you say you can't, you don't know
who you are. You don't know the greatness that is in you.

Someone has said that the Bible is not so much about
God but about man in the presence of God. We know a lot
about man standing in God's presence. Man in God's
presence is really magnificent, even with his sinfulness.
Jesus calls us to potential greatness, especially in the area
of forgiveness.

"What sacrifice will I make to the Lord for all that he
has done for me?" The psalmist says, "I will give you a
broken heart." My brothers and sisters, this call to
forgiveness is really a key to our prolonged and on-going
life together. It is bound up very much with our understanding of our own sinfulness. How can anyone who has
really sinned and knows that he or she is a sinner, not
forgive? How can we possibly withhold mercy and
calculate and measure? It is not the time for calculating, it
is not the time for measuring. It is the time for throwing
our heart at the feet of Christ and by that act changing the
world, as Jesus did. If we call on the name of Jesus who
died for us and forgave when he didn't have to forgive, we
will also be able to forgive. In his name, I call upon you
now, and always, for the rest of our lives, to forgive one
another as God has forgiven us. And if we are forgiving,
there is nothing that can harm us—nothing.

"Am I the Answer to Someone's Prayer?"

I was reading the story of Susanna from the Book of
Daniel today in the poustinia. I'm sure you are familiar
with it. Susanna, a very beautiful woman, is unjustly accused by two elders of infidelity. She pleads her innocence

before the people, but to no avail. She cried to the Lord, but seemingly received no answer. As she was actually being led away to be killed—well, let's listen to it in the words of scripture: *"The Lord heard her cry and, as she was being led away to die, he roused the Holy Spirit residing in a young man named Daniel who began to shout: 'I am innocent of this woman's blood!"* (13, 44-45).

I can't tell you how much these words struck me. I think they have a profound significance for our life together.

Sometimes others are in a helpless situation. It doesn't mean that they are themselves afraid to act, though this might be the case. But often, like Susanna, they have done everything within their powers. Still, because of circumstances, they remain helpless, trapped. They have come to the end of their ability to free themselves. All they have left is the strength to cry to the Lord.

And God, we know, hears our prayers. The lesson from the Susanna story is that God often hears that cry by *inspiring someone else to speak up for them,* or to help in some way not open to the one in difficulty. *We often are God's answer to someone else's prayer.* God rouses our "holy spirit," that deepest part of us which is sensitive to the plight of our brothers and sisters. If we are aware of their plight, that already may be the beginning of God's response to their prayer.

There is an incident in the novel about the Quakers, *The Peaceable Kingdom,* which illustrates this very well. Margaret Fall, one of the early followers of George Fox, the founder of Quakerism, had been taken into the dungeon of an English prison to "bring her back to reality." She saw small children being tortured and even hung. She fled from the prison to confront George Fox with her pangs of doubt. She asked him to prove to her the existence of a God of love in the face of all this misery. He replied: "Stop crying for a proof of God's love! Prove it thyself! How else dost thou think He can manifest His love? In the case of those children in the cage, about to be hanged, it is *thou* He touched: All He has to reach those children is *thee!*"

This struck me very forcibly. God sometimes hears other peoples' prayers by inspiring someone else to act. May our "holy spirits" be awake and ready for such touches of the Lord.

Rejoicing In Truth and Goodness

My brothers and sisters, when God reveals to us the dark and unredeemed areas of our hearts, this is his love and mercy. He desires us to be filled with his life and love, and he cannot accomplish this work unless he reveals to us the unloving and lifeless spaces. One message of the Scriptures is a harsh saying, and it is this: there is a part of our heart which wishes to kill goodness and truth in other people. We say: "Not I, Lord, surely, not I." But if we are honest with ourselves we will admit that this is part of the "mystery of iniquity" in us.

"Nothing bothers us so much as other people's virtues," said Mark Twain. We wonder how it is that people wanted to kill a man like Jesus, who was so good and kind and merciful. What a mystery this is! The answer is: Goodness, real goodness, threatens us, shows up our own lives. We must stamp it out at all costs. It is this revulsion for goodness which drove Jesus' enemies to seek to kill him.

We cannot stand too much goodness! This reaction is in

all of us; to what degree only God knows. We must yearn and plead for the grace to rejoice in the truth and in the goodness of others. One day the disciples went out to preach. They came back complaining that others were preaching in the Lord's name too but they "were not of our closed group." Jesus just shrugged his shoulders and said, "So what! What does it matter? If they're not against you, they're for you. As long as the Gospel is preached."

St. Paul expresses a similar thought: As long as Christ is preached. He would rejoice in whomever did it. He remarked in another place: "Whatever is good and holy and beautiful and just, think about these things." I think he also meant that whenever you come upon those things, rejoice. It is the work of the Father. Jesus did not come just so that *I* might be good, preach the Gospel, etc., but that *everybody* might do these things. We must learn to rejoice in goodness, wherever God brings it forth.

The reason for this resistance in our hearts is the same reason for most of our other ills! God is not the Center of our lives, of our consciousness, of our striving. *We* are. Thus we tend to see everything in relation to ourselves instead of to God. Instead of seeing goodness and truth as a work of God, we tend to see it as detracting from our own worth. We find it hard to rejoice because *we* didn't do it. The glory of others detracts from our own glory. We, and not God, are the center of our enterprise.

Likewise, when people praise us for some really good thing we have done or a gift we possess, if we're trying to "be humble," we tend to be embarrassed by compliments. We are embarrassed for the same reason that we take offense at the goodness of others: God is not the center of the enterprise. *We* are. If God were central we would see such praise as acknowledgment of the gifts and wonders of God in us. We are embarrassed because we still really believe we are the source of the gifts. Our embarrassment should be a signal to us that we still do not see things in relation to God. The truest thing we can say when complimented is, "Thanks be to God," or "Praise the Lord." This doesn't mean that I miss seeing my achievement, but it acknowledges that God really is the source of the gifts, and I give the honor to him.

My brothers and sisters, this rejoicing in the goodness of others is very important because Jesus died for goodness and truth and life—not just mine but everyone's. When I "gnash my teeth" interiorly at goodness in others I do exactly what the people in the Gospel did: I seek to kill Jesus. I seek to stamp out the truth and the light because they detract, (so I think) from my own goodness. We must beware of this attitude lest we continue to crucify the Lord anew in our own hearts.

"Are You One of These?"

A few days ago I received a letter, or rather a copy of something, as there was only a name and one comment on the article. It was an excerpt from a private revelation of Our Lady to Mary of Agreda; the book from which it was taken is called *City of God*. The excerpt sent to me concerns the sins of the clergy. One of the passages reads:

> If the pastors and the chiefs of the house of the Lord seek only a life of ease, without caring to engage in true earnest labor, they will make themselves account able for the ruin of the flock of Christ and for the car-

nage brought on by the infernal wolves. O my daughter, into what a lamentable state has the Christian people been cast by the powerful, by the pastors and by the wicked ministers whom God has given them in his secret judgments! O what confusion and chastisement await them! Before the tribunal of the just Judge they will have no excuse; since the Catholic truth undeceives them, their conscience loudly protests, while they willfully remain deaf to all warnings.

After this passage there is a notation by the sender: "Are *you* one of these priests?"

By the grace of God, when I read this comment there was only a *brief* stirring within me of a whole complex of reactions with which I'm sure you are familiar: "What gall to send this to *me*." "The poor, misguided soul; one of those reactionary Catholics." "Imagine, accusing *me* of such things."

I say, this reaction lasted only a brief moment. Then I caught myself (or rather was caught by the Lord) and realized that the whole weight of the interior discussion had shifted from me to the sender. I read the excerpt again. The sender was right. I *am* one of those priests. To what extent, with what damage to the Church and to myself, only God knows. But it is true, I am one of those.

I wrote back to the sender and said: "Yes, I am one of those priests, guilty in some measure (God alone knows) of all the sins Our Lady talks about. All of us, priests and laity, must strive harder to do penance and live the Gospel, so that Jesus and Mary may be more loved."

My brothers and sisters, I don't know how artificial or

unreal my sentiments sound; I believe they are part of me.
I know they are certainly the ideal towards which I should
strive. Because, as I prayed about it afterwards, the Lord
seemed to be saying that this is what conversion is really all
about. That, when we are criticized, or taken to task for
something—especially by one another—our first reactions
should not be resentment, offense, hurt, etc. By the grace
of God, our spontaneous movement should be, "I am one
of them," or to paraphrase David to Nathan: "I am the
man."

Believe me, I know how unreal all this sounds. But I
think it's the ideal conversion of heart to which the Lord
calls us. In our life with God, the spontaneous movement
to admit we are sinners is the safest ground we can be on.
Part of our anxieties stem from our fear that other people
will discover our faults, our sins, our secret infidelities.
The saints' answer to that was: "Yes, I am one of these."
"Yes, I am a sinner." "Yes, I am the man." Then their
lives were built on the mercy of God and not on subter-
fuge, deceit, facades and the playing of games with God.

I am not advocating "truth sessions," where we go
around making all our faults known to everyone. No. It's
an attitude of heart I'm speaking about, a spontaneous admission of sinfulness instead of a spontaneous line of
defense and barrage of justifications aimed at our accuser.

"In many things we all offend." If I haven't done what I
am being accused of, I've done something else that I've
gotten away with, that's never come to light. If I haven't
done what I'm being accused of, at some time I probably
have *wanted* to do it! If we are convinced that we are sinners—have accepted the fact with all our hearts—we can

always find a reason for accepting criticism. There is always some level or dimension in us that needs to be further purified.

Our lives must be built and must rest on the mercy of God. Jesus does not say, "The kingdom of God has come. Shape up!" What Jesus asks for is that we admit our *need* for him. Jesus never refused people who really needed him and *admitted* that need. Jesus asks for *repentance.*

I don't know what's happening in the heart of my friend who sent me that excerpt. I pray that he or she acted out of real concern for God's honor and kingdom. My responsibility is how I allow that letter to affect my heart. By the grace of God, it has made me more aware of how I've wasted and continue to waste the graces of the priesthood. God have mercy on me. I am one of them. Pray for me.

Do We Want To Be Healed?

There is a significant feature in the Gospel story of the paralytic. Picture the scene. Jesus is in a room of people and suddenly the roof opens and this man is lowered down. We would expect Jesus to say, "He's come to be healed. Be healed and get up." But that's not exactly the order of things. The first thing that Jesus looks at is a deeper wound. The first thing that Jesus says is, "Your sins are forgiven." The eyes of Christ are focused on the deepest wounds in him. And only afterwards does he heal his body.

In the Charismatic Renewal there is a similar practice. Before people are prayed over for healing, they are asked to forgive anyone that they might have anything against. In the Scriptures, there is a very intimate connection between the wounds in our hearts and the other evils we experience. One of the deepest notions in the whole Bible is that the evils around us and in us are caused by our broken relationship with God.

This understanding is reflected in the very first story of Genesis. The author looked around his life situation, and he saw that women have pains of childbirth; he also saw that man had difficulty making a living, and he said: "Where do these pains come from?" His answer was: "We have broken our relationship with God."

The Psalmist does not pray, "Lord, heal my body." He prays, "Lord, heal my *soul.*" Man always attempts to cure himself by curing the superficial things in his life. Our modern society is a good example of how frustrating that effort really is. The theory is that if we all had enough to eat and enough good things to occupy ourselves with, we would be happy. We know that it is not so.

One of the deepest truths of revelation about ourselves and our situation is that the problem is our relationship with God. Who can number all the hurts caused by our interrelationships with people and the ramifications of those hatreds on our body and psyche? We talk about psychosomatic medicine, a very familiar concept: There's something broken inside of us and it reacts on our body and we even become physically sick because things inside are not well-ordered. Our relationship with God is the most important thing. Why don't we straighten it out then?

There is a story of a woman who was a paralytic in bed for fifteen years, and the cure for her disease was finally discovered. But she didn't want it! She had become accustomed to her sickness and to be cured would have changed her whole life. She didn't want to get out of bed.

I think that we are like that woman. We are more at home with our disease. Even though it hurts us, it is something that we can manage. We're familiar with it. But we don't know what total health would be like, and that frightens us. We'd have to get out of bed. We haven't explored a lot of those regions beyond our sick room and we're not so sure we want to.

And so, the deeper problem is not so much *how* we become healed, but *do we want to be healed?* Do we want to get out of bed? Deep down, I think we realize that God truly can heal us, but we know that if we choose God, we're going to have to give up everything else for that healing. All the other pills on our bed table comforted us, even though for fifteen years they never *did* heal us. But we liked them. We know that if we choose God, we might have to throw all the other pills away and get up. We're not so sure that we want to. We're even afraid of the Doctor! How can we be healed if we fear the Doctor? We won't even let him come into the room.

Another fear we have is that if we choose God, we're going to be unable to do and choose a lot of things, and that's exactly right! We cannot avoid making absolute choices. In fact, it's choices that give our lives meaning. To make definite choices, to choose this and not to choose that, is one of the deepest lessons of life that we all have to learn, and failure to choose is to be nowhere. It's not to be zeroed in on any value or any real meaning. And that's what we're afraid of too. We're afraid of choosing God lest we have nothing else.

But what Jesus tells us, and the lives of the saints reveal to us, is that, if we can make that absolute choice for God, somehow everything else will be returned to us as on the first day of creation.

One of Gandhi's favorite sayings was that the "whole of creation is the garment of God, and if you can let it go it will be returned to you." That's the act that we're reluctant to make. Jesus told us that if we give everything away, it will be returned to us. But we have to give it away first. We have to have this longing for healing that is absolute. Saint Paul tells us that with Jesus there was no "yes" and "no" or "maybe." We can't lay in our sick-bed and think that "maybe" we want to be cured or "perhaps." It has to be yes or no. And the same Spirit that was in Jesus, the same Spirit that raised Jesus from the dead, is in us. That same Spirit gives us the power to say our Yes as loudly and as clearly as Jesus did.

That might seem a little extreme. But Jesus has come to make us total sons and daughters of the Father. That power is in us if we want to be healed.

When we raise up the gifts at Mass and we say, "Through Him and with Him and in Him," people answer with the great Amen. The word in Hebrew for Amen has the same connotation as righteousness, like "That's right"—"we agree with that." It's a way of affirming that we want to be as right with God as Jesus was, and that through these gifts, the bread and wine that will be changed into his Body and Blood, in the power of that Food, we can get up out of our sick-beds. Even if we've been there for fifteen years and we're afraid of the world outside, we can do it in the strength of that Food.

And so, the same Lord who forgave this man's sins and gave him the power to pick up his bed and walk is present with us. That's not poetry; it's not a pious belief; it's the foundation of our faith. The Risen Lord is present with us. So, with everything that is in us, let us say Yes and reach out to him and ask him to help us get out of bed, to be impelled by his Spirit to move and to help him heal the world that needs him so much.

Letting Go

Several days after my father died I went to the cemetery to visit the graves of my mother and father. I sat down on the grass, and I thought how these two people had come together in bodily union, how I had flowed forth from them. Now they were gone and I continue on.

I think the Lord gave me a real experience of "letting them go." He taught me not to consider this as anti-life, or anti-world or a rejection, but a letting go, because someday we're going to have to let everything go. And so I let my parents go, gave them back to God.

In that moment, I realized that something so precious as those two lives must be preserved in God forever; that nothing of *that* value, of that good, can ever really be lost. I realized that somehow, God would cherish everything in our lives that is good and holy and true. He'll keep it forever, in a new way.

As I sat there in the cemetery I experienced both a dying and a rising in relation to my parents. I "released them" into God and in that act knew that they really were in God.

I share that with you because I think that, as we go on, we're going to experience more and more those three movements; letting things go, letting them go to God, and realizing that we too, are going to be carried along into him in some new and wonderful way.

Advent People

I think the spirit of Advent more closely approximates our ordinary Christian life: we are not sinners who need complete conversion; nor are we completely Easter people—the Resurrection hasn't fully taken over in our lives. We are more like Advent people: we're "becoming" people, we're hoping people, we're people longing for Jesus to come more and more completely into our lives.

One of the themes in the Scripture is Judgment. What is Judgment? Judgment is the vision we get of ourselves when we are confronted with God's truth, especially in the life of Christ. Judgment is the contortions we go through inside when the truth hits us right in the face and we have to make a decision as to which way we are going to turn. At the end of our lives, Judgment will be a little more tragic because then it will be God leaving us to our own desires. Can you imagine that thought? God won't bother us any more. At the end of the world, he will leave us to our own desires wherever we are. To our desires that are twisted. To our desires that are halfway straightened out, or almost completely straightened out. At the end, God will leave us alone. And that will be our Judgment.

But now we are in the time of Mercy and, thanks be to God, he keeps bothering us, he keeps after us, he won't let us rest. He keeps reminding us, "I'm coming" and asking "What is your attitude to my coming? Are you simply *waiting* for me or do you *want* me to come?" They're not the same thing. "Are you simply passing the days, waiting, or do you long for the days to be complete?"

My brothers and sisters, there is no new future without change of heart. Some people repeat the same day over again; that's different from growing. There is no new exciting future unless we cooperate with the Lord in wanting to change. For the Christian, time means "approaching Christ." Time has nothing more to do with one day coming after another, or one month following another; this is pagan time. For us, time is "approaching Jesus." History is no longer a straight line—it is a convergence into Christ who is the Center of all time.

Our religion is a religion of promise. Without God's promises, the history of Israel has no meaning. For us, life is exciting because God is our future. He tells us, "Don't be afraid to step into the future because that's where I am."

What is it that holds us back from Christ? A lot of things that hold us back from God are in our past. It is good to pray for the complete healing of our past, to ask Christ to come and heal us from our past hurts, our psychic problems, everything in us that says "No, Lord, don't come now—not yet." Yes, we want Jesus to heal us of everything that is in us so that we cry, "Yes, come now—and hurry, please!"

The coming of Christ is often a time of turmoil. Sometimes he comes gently. But sometimes he comes and stirs everything up—like the Baptist preaching in the wilderness. When people saw him and heard him, they probably asked themselves, "My God, what's happening? Is it the end of the world? Who is this guy? He's a fanatic!"

Sometimes the word comes in that way and we think it's the end of something. We think that our life is going over the precipice. But instead, very often, in this kind of coming, something new is being born.

There is a story of an American who went to climb his

first mountain in Switzerland. He had never climbed a mountain, and the day before, he was camping at the foot of the mountain. At about 5:00 A.M. there was a fantastic rumbling and roaring all through the canyon. He shot up and said, "Oh, my goodness, what's happening? It sounds like the end of the world!" His guide next to him woke up and heard this enormous rumbling and crashing, but he knew what it was. In the morning the ice on the mountain starts to melt, and there is a great shifting of the ice so it sounds like an avalanche coming down. So the guide just yawned and said, "No, it isn't the end of the world—it's just the beginning of a new day."

Very often, when the Lord comes with this rumbling into our lives, we think, "Oh goodness, it's the end of the world." But it just might be for us the beginning of a new day.

Waiting Without Idols

Most of you know who Caryll Houselander was. She was a famous English Catholic lay woman. In many of her books she portrayed a great sensitivity to the pain of God—the pain of Christ. A friend went to visit her one day and found Caryll on the floor writhing in pain. Her friend asked her what was the matter and she said that she had just received this letter from a friend of hers, and she could tell by her handwriting that she was suffering a great deal. Caryll was on the floor experiencing that person's pain.

The pain of Christ arises from our worshiping of false idols. We should pray to be able to feel something of the longing of Christ for us to get rid of all the idols that are around: "I will heal their disloyalties, I will love them with all my heart. What has Ephraim to do with idols any more, when it is I who hear his prayer and care for him?''

We should try to hear Christ saying those words to us: ''What has Ephraim to do with idols any more?'' Somebody has said, ''Until the Lord comes, how can we wait without idols?'' We have to fashion something, hold onto something, until the real Lord comes.

How can we purify our hearts? By living the same rhythm Jesus lived: prayer and service. Somehow in this rhythm, back and forth, God will educate us. He will teach us. In our neighbor we will come to understand God better, and in our prayer alone, we will get deeper insights into who our neighbor really is.

So let us keep prayng for one another and keep striving to cleanse our hearts and get ready for the coming of our *real* Lord when all the false idols will vanish and we will see him face to face.

Keep On Praying

For quite some time now I have been praying for a deeper realization of the connection between my prayer and the needs of the world. My heart seems so stony in the face of the suffering, confusion and meaninglessness which are part of the lives of so many people. At times I feel like a person watching an apartment building burning with people inside, and I am standing by, quite unmoved and unsympathetic. I want somehow to experience more the seriousness of the situation.

I hadn't prayed for this for several weeks, then, all of a sudden, the gift came. The touches of the finger of God often happen like this. They come when you're not looking, when you'd almost forgotten about it; then they sneak in the back door of your heart.

Catherine related the story once of how George, her son, had been cured many years ago. She had found out that Father Paul of Graymoor had spent hours in prayer for George's recovery. I had heard the story before, and many similar stories. But God moved this time. I asked myself if I too believed in the power of prayer like Father Paul, and if I did, why didn't I pray more for people. "Look at all the needs of people," I said to myself. "Do you really believe your prayer can help those situations?"

That day and the days which followed, something began to happen in my heart. It wasn't simply a deeper intellectual conviction. Some new dimension opened up inside—a deeper faith in the power of prayer. There was a deeper conviction that my prayer was really being heard.

All during these past three days, needs of people the world over kept coming to mind in a way that has never happened before. They were detailed and explicit, and accompanying all of them was this realization that God was asking me to pray, and that he was listening—that "connections" were being made.

I prayed for all the people in town. I prayed for lonely people that God might reveal himself to them. I prayed for young people that they might find God. I prayed for people who sought God in alcohol, drugs, and in the million and one other ways which lead nowhere. I prayed for the Jews that they might come to know Christ in faith. I prayed for those working toward Christian unity at all levels. I prayed for people in parishes who, if they were reading a notice about attending an inter-faith service this week, might be moved to go. I prayed for the millions who have no meaning in their lives. I made a circuit around the world and prayed for people sleeping, those just getting up, those going to work, those working, those coming home, those going to bed. I can't recall all the people I prayed for this week. Each prayer was more specific, and accompanied by a stranger conviction of being heard than I've ever experienced.

I don't always pray for these people. But the intentions kept coming into my heart. I felt as if God were dictating these needs, and that he wanted me to pray for them. I was sure that he was listening. Something new has happened. I feel that God is calling me to a life of deeper intercession. Pray for me that I am faithful to this movement of the Spirit.

I guess, then, my word to you is this: that prayer does change things, prayer can touch people's lives, and that God wants us to pray more, to intercede more for others. The needs are endless. Do we really believe our prayer can help people? God helped me to believe in the power of prayer just a little more. I will pray that your faith in prayer increases also.

Meditation While Sorting Holy Pictures

Recently I was looking for a project to do in the poustinia. I mentioned this to Catherine. She suggested that I help sort the thousands of holy cards she has been collecting for the religious museum. I don't know how much of the following inspirations are due entirely to this sorting, but I know that as I sorted there descended upon me a whole atmosphere of thoughts, feelings and attitudes—attitudes not wholly new but with a new level of appreciation about them. It is this "atmosphere of attitudes" that I wish to share with you.

What was I sorting? Pictures of Our Lord and of Our Lady of every imaginable type. Pictures of the Saints, some of whom I had never heard about. Pictures of St. Joseph and of the Angels. Cards with quotations from the Bible and from the writings of the Saints and holy people of God. Prayer cards with countless dedications and aspirations and petitions.

As I sorted these cards for hours on end I felt drawn more intimately into the company of the people whom they represented. I began to live, in that sorting corner, more familiarly with Jesus and Mary and the Saints. I found myself stopping frequently to read a prayer or to make an act of consecration. I read about numerous revelations and apparitions. I reread, after many years, the promises of the Sacred Heart to St. Margaret Mary and the pleas of Mary to the children at Fatima. I read about many of the private appearances of Jesus and Mary to their chosen ones.

What I found myself immersed in, in a new way, was the world of piety and devotion of God's people. Passing through my hands were the heart-beats of Jesus and Mary, and the responses of their children. Yes, these were sacred cards flowing through my fingers, many of them torn and worn due to many years' use. In some real sense these cards and pictures represented the heart of the Church, because they were the prayers of God's people. I was handling the life-blood of hearts. While sorting, I found myself living more and more in a very personal world, peopled by these residents of heaven. It was not an entirely new experience, but there was something deeper, more real, more immediate about it all.

This overflowed into my daily life. In my prayers I found myself using more often the ejaculations and prayers on these cards. I was re-discovering some of the value of recited prayers after a few years of relying pretty much on my own imagination and ingenuity.

I found myself reciting litanies and saying the rosary more frequently. In short, I found myself returning to many of the prayer-forms and styles that had been part of my life before the Council. What meaning and beauty I am re-discovering in the Litany of the Sacred Heart and the litany of Our Lady! At the present time I am finding new inspiration in these prayers.

But more has happened. As I re-read the account of the revelations of Our Lord and of Our Lady I was struck by what was a constant theme in all of them: the Hearts of Jesus and Mary are suffering from the sins, the coldness, and the indifference of people. Further, many people are walking the road to eternal chaos, and Jesus and Mary plead for prayer and penance in order to save them.

My brothers and sisters, I believe that one of the particular graces I received was a greater realization that there is a tremendous battle taking place for the hearts of mankind. Yes, there is a battle, and the Lord needs our prayers and our sacrifices and our love to assist him in his work of salvation. One of our greatest dignities is to share with him in this saving work. I found myself being tempered and drawn a little bit farther away from any kind of Pollyanna view of the world. The Saints do not tire from telling us that complete joy is reserved for heaven, and that now is the time for putting our shoulders to the task of helping Jesus in his salvific work.

We are made for joy and for love, but such joy and love

must be built on the truth. In our present situation the truth is that many people are walking towards personal destruction. The truth is that we can assist the Lord in his work of reaching these hearts. The truth is that Jesus and Mary need our prayers, our sacrifices, and our love. The Lord taught me that whatever rejoicing comes my way must never be allowed to drown out the cries of those whose eternal destiny hangs in the balance. As long as we journey towards the Father, may all our joys be tempered by the realization that there are many who live without God; and, may all our sorrows be tempered by the joy we have in knowing that Jesus is using our lives in his mission of salvation.

The Wonderful Gift of Faith

Around Christmastime one year I went to visit my sister who was then teaching fourth grade, and she decided to put on for me one of the acts of the Christmas play she was preparing. So I sat in the back of the room and soon the three Kings started making their way up the aisle. The first little kid said, "What is that in yonder sky?" And the other kid was so nervous he forgot his lines and said, "I don't know!"

We are all kings and queens. Some know what the star is all about, and some don't. And the difference is—our faith. The Church says, in one of her orations, that just as the star was a light for the Kings, so our faith is a light to God. I began to think of the great gift that faith is. Without faith there would be no epiphanies at all. Without faith, there would be no manifestations of God in our lives. There might be manifestations, but *not for us.*

There are some gifts that open up to us an infinite variety of gifts. If someone gave me a pair of ice skates for Christmas, that's wonderful, but I can't eat them or take them to a concert! But if someone gave me $100.00 and said, ''Buy whatever you like,'' that opens up a whole variety of gifts. It is the same with the gift of faith: Faith opens to us the whole universe that God made.

What would our lives be like without faith? Without faith, we would not know what it is to pray. Without faith, we would not know if God was for us or against us. Without faith, we would have no living relationship with God. It's hard to imagine, isn't it?

Without faith, we would not have a living relationship with Jesus. His words would not have life for us. Without faith, his death would be just another one of the tragedies of the world—a man was killed for some reason or other; we don't know exactly why. Without faith, there would be no resurrection. We would not be sure of life after death. Without faith, there would be no Blessed Virgin Mary. We might have heard her name in one of the stories of the Gospel, but without faith we could not talk to Mary. She would not be able to instruct us about Jesus.

Without faith there would be no angels and saints. No Francis of Assisi. No Brother Juniper nor Brother Leo. No Augustine, no Thomas Aquinas. At least, they would not mean for us what they mean now.

What would our lives be without faith? What would we be doing? What would our lives be *for*? Who would be our Love, and what would our loves be?

St. Paul says that this gift is for everybody. That's part of the mystery. God wants everybody to share in his new life. And it's God's plan that somehow each of us is to fulfill the prophecy of Isaiah. With faith in our own hearts he wants us to "rise and shine out, for his light has come." The glory of the Lord is rising on *me*. And though night still covers the earth, above *you* the Lord now rises, and above *you* his glory appears. All are assembled and coming toward *you*. The nations come to *your* light, and kings to *your* dawning brightness. God wants each of us to be his shining light through the great gift of our faith.

What can we give God in return if not our faith-response? We must work with God. We have to do our part. We have to *want* to believe. We must want to *be* this light for others. Let us really praise God for our faith, one of the greatest gifts that we have. Without it, Jesus would have come and all the rest of it, but he would not be Lord *for us*.

"What is that in yonder sky?" Through the gift of our faith we shout with joy, "We know, we know!"

The Only Real Revolution

There has only been one revolution that has ever really changed the world: The revolution of personal love for your neighbor. Try as we might to shape up the world in other ways by joining this group or getting involved in that political movement, there never has been any other way to change the world for God except to love the person next to us. Because that's the most difficult thing, we use every kind of dodge to avoid it.

The Christian is called to confront man with his lack of love for God. The problem of the world at the deepest level is that man has not turned towards God. And so—how do you turn man towards God? What do you do, really?

What do you join? How do you act? What do you say?
The only revolution that has ever worked is to love the person next to you and hope that somehow, that person will
love the person next to him.

Let us get on our knees and beg God that we never
forget the heart of that revolution. That we never forget
that the only unconditional thing that God has called us to
is to love the person next to us, whatever color, size or
shape. That is the revolution. And let us pray that we never
rationalize ourselves out of this truth. Let us pray that we
never think that some other kind of organization, some
other political body, that anything else will ever really do
it—because other things have been tried and failed.

About Waiting

One of the manifestations of original sin in us is our in-
ability to wait. Poor little creatures that we are, we are
disoriented from God and we think that we can do a lot
more than we can, especially in the deep things of the
heart. We see a flower growing and we wish it would grow
faster. But a flower has to obey the rhythm of life that God
has put into it. We are impatient, and so we try to work out
somehow for ourselves our salvation, those deep heart
things that we know we can't live without.

I would like to invite you to enter into the heart of the
woman who, because she was without sin, knew how to
wait perfectly. Mary was the person who did not try to
manipulate anybody, and especially not God, did not try
to work out her own salvation in her own time the way she
wanted it to happen. Mary belonged to that little group of
people, the *anawim,* who waited for hundreds and hun-

dreds of years, and finally the waiting came to a point of perfection in Mary. Her waiting brought down the Word of God. She waited for God and God came into her womb.

Then, after Jesus was born, Mary waited for him to grow up. She didn't try and force him into some mold. She had to wait for wisdom and grace to manifest itself in the life of Jesus. When Jesus went out into his public life, Mary often had to wait for him to come home so she could see him. Mary had to stand at the Cross and wait for Jesus to die. She had to wait for the Father's time when he finally took the life of her Son and ended his sufferings.

And then, Mary waited for Jesus to come back to life again. What must that waiting have been after the death of Jesus! Our reaction would be: "It didn't happen the way we thought it would happen, and now we have to do something." But Mary waited and trusted that God would do something. She waited and God raised Jesus back to life again.

Mary waited with the apostles for the Spirit to come, and he did come. Mary waited to return to Jesus, to see him again in heaven next to his Father. And now, Mary waits for all of us. Her perfection of waiting was so powerful that it brought God to earth and made all God's plans come true for her because she knew how not to manipulate him, how to let him really be God, and to let him act in her life. She waited so perfectly that God could do anything he wanted with her.

I invite you to enter into the mystery of Mary's waiting. Someone asked me once what he could do for Advent, and I said, "You could learn how to wait better." As you think of Mary's waiting and your own waiting, think of God's waiting for you. Our waiting is simply the echo in our own hearts of God's infinite waiting for us. God waits and waits and waits for us to come to him.

We praise the power of God's grace in Mary—she who knew how to wait perfectly so that God's plan could be perfectly fulfilled in her.

Mary, Queen of Our Hearts

The total mystery of Jesus is always present to us. Whether we're in the chapel, or walking outside, or wherever we are, the whole mystery of Jesus is present, *but we are not present to him.* In the liturgy, in our loving of one another, in our life, what we are trying to do is assimilate little by little the image of Christ, which is God's plan for each of us.

Every feast that we celebrate has a particular grace, a particular growth in the life of Jesus that God wants to give us. I prayed today: "Lord, what is the grace of the Queenship of Mary? I mean, what should the Queenship of Mary mean for me?" The answer I received was something like this: that after Jesus, Mary should be the most important person in our life of faith.

Why? Because, if we're trying to become like Jesus, which we are, we must realize that Mary is the most important person *in his life.* So this primacy of Mary, this role of Mary in our lives, is simply reflecting what is part of the heart of Jesus himself. Jesus loves Mary his mother more than any other human being. And if we have decided to become like him, she also should have this place, this primacy in our hearts.

Now that might sound a bit extreme. We know that often people have difficulty with Mary. Sometimes they feel that Catholics give her too much importance, or talk about her in extravagant terms. I was wondering, how can we explain this?

Imagine if you met Jesus and Mary walking towards you. Now, you have to move somehow. How are you going to greet them? We know in our hearts that Jesus is God, and that him only can we worship and adore. But try to imagine both of them there together. Try to sort out in your heart where admiration and awe for Mary stops and adoration for Jesus begins. We know there's a difference. But what would we say to Jesus that we wouldn't say to Mary? It's something like that, that when we're in the presence of Jesus and Mary, we get all mixed up and we can't sort out what kind of label to put on this kind of awe, and what label to put on that one. We know the difference theologically, but in our expressions of love and in our attitudes, in our prayer life, the lines sometimes blur.

So very simply, if that is true for Jesus, that Mary holds this place in his heart, the question I put to you for your own prayer life is, "Does she have that kind of place for you? Is she somehow Queen there?"

Mary As Teacher of the Gospel

I asked Mary for a word today. We ask Our Lord for a word; but I don't think we often ask Our Lady. She said, "Tell them that if they're searching for a way to understand the Scriptures, tell them that before they meditate on the Scriptures, enter my heart and I will teach them."

We have only a few hundred words of Jesus in the Gospels, very few really. Consider: Mary heard the first word of Jesus, and the last, and she heard thousands and thousands of words from his lips all during his life. In Mary's heart are thousands of meditations from the lips of Jesus. She said to me, "If you want to really understand the Gospel, enter here and I will teach you."

Imagine the life in Nazareth. Jesus must have often rehearsed, in a way, what he was going to say publicly. Mary meditated on these things. When she heard Jesus talk publicly, she probably was not hearing too many new words. Mary had years and years of time in Nazareth to think about all the things that one day would be in the Gospel. Anything at all that Jesus said entered into Mary's heart. Her Immaculate Heart was transparent to God's grace; there were no obstacles to her understanding.

If you want to know what sin is, or why Jesus had to suffer so much, enter Mary's heart, because in her very *purity* she knows what sin is, more than any living human being. So with all the words of Scripture: her heart is able to translate for us, amplify for us, clarify for us, the Word of God.

Very simply, that is the word I share with you today. I know myself that I'm going to use that method more. I invite you to try it also because Mary has thousands of words of Jesus in her heart; she has pondered them with awesome clarity. Who knows and understands better the Word of God? Who could be a better teacher?

Visiting

I would like to offer for your consideration one aspect of Mary's great soul, one delicate touch of her relationships with people. It is that very human and beautiful phenomenon we call *visiting*.

At first mention, it does not sound like anything too heroic. Don't we all visit our friends, and like to do so, and don't we do it often? Perhaps this is true of our close friends: we do not need to be invited twice. But what about people we do not know too well?

Take the example of a new neighbor moving in. We watch them move in, wonder who they are, think to ourselves how nice it would be to visit them (or perhaps we don't even get that far!). More often than not we will end up not visiting, having explained it away somehow as not necessary, not the right time, too embarrassing for them, etc., etc.

The fact is that visiting in such situations requires something of the quality of humility. Do not important people have visitors? To become a visitor is to enter a kind of self-emptying state of soul. It's an admission of dependency of sorts. An admission of need. We say by our visit that we need friends and want them, and are willing to seek them out. Self-sufficient people do not need to visit.

Or consider the situation in a community. There are people we would like to know better—really believe we should know better—but how do we go about it? One way is to go and visit them, invite them out for a walk, or just talk and get to know them better. If you think that is easy, just try it, especially with someone whom you have never invited for a walk before, or tried to sit down and visit with.

In community, where we have roles and functions, there is a tendency to treat people first in their job capacity as office clerk, kitchen worker, businessman, and so forth. We also tend to treat our superiors in their role as "permission-hander-outer" or advice giver. Try sometime just to visit—not want anything or ask anything—but just visit, and see how they are doing.

I remember, as a parish priest, I used to go around and visit homes. I wasn't after any money, or trying to sign people up for committees. I really just wanted to visit. Most people were very apprehensive until they found out that I really did come just to see how they were doing.

All this may not seem to have much to do with Our Lady, but I believe it does. When communications had broken down, the Lord came to visit us. He took the first step toward friendship. In Mary's visit to her cousin, Elizabeth was surprised. She exclaimed "What are you doing visiting me when it is I who should be visiting you!" Mary is a good model for us in this matter. It takes a special kind of defenselessness and delicacy to be a good visitor, to simply approach someone out of a real desire to know them better and not for any "useful" purpose.

We could ask Our Lady to obtain for us this same grace—this same graciousness—to be a good visitor. Ask for the humility to take another step in getting to know better your brothers and sisters. Evidently, Mary and Elizabeth were or became real friends: They stayed together for three months. Sometimes we cannot imagine ourselves with a certain person beyond a few nervous minutes. It may simply be because we have never taken the time to visit them. Mary, patroness of visitors, ask your Son for this grace for us too, to be good visitors with one another!

Oh Jesus, That's My Way!

I wish to share a few thoughts about the person who is called the greatest saint in the modern world. That's saying an awful lot. There are some people who have never heard of St. Therese. If it had been up to her, she would have lived and died completely unknown.

The first thing I'd like to share is that we should stand in awe of the incredible marvel of grace that God worked in her. Her vocation was somehow to discover and live what pure love is. We think of loving God in many different ways. Somehow, for St. Therese, her vocation was to discover the actual nature of love. She said: "I see my call to *be* love." I don't know about you, but I don't very often think of really *being* love.

We think of *loving* Jesus in different ways. We love him in the poor. We love him in service. But what is the essence of love? God called her in a way to *be love*. She finally could not desire any of the things that are almost necessary to love—to be known, to do great things for God. They are O.K., but somehow she wanted to go *beyond* those things. She approached very closely the essence of loving.

But it's really important for us not to try to become like Therese, not to try to become like anybody else. We can learn a lot from her love, and that's why God revealed her to us. But part of the meaning of her life for us is that she was faithful to *her* way, her very own way.

One day she cried, "Oh Jesus! That's it! That's my way!" It was not the way of any other saint, any other person that she'd ever read about. She said, "Jesus—that's my life."

My brothers and sisters, God calls each one of us in a unique and individual way that is the way of no other person and never will be. I pray for you that some day soon in your search for Jesus, in your search for the answer to the question, "How am *I* supposed to come to him?" you'll

say, "Oh Jesus! That's it! That's for me!" And if you
follow that individual way that God is calling you to, you'll
come to Christ and he'll transform you. You have to
believe that. God does not want you to copy anybody exactly. You can learn from everybody. But if you believe in
your own call in your own heart, he'll come to you. That's
what Therese did. "Jesus! Jesus! That's it! That's my own
call!"

That is the grace that I ask for you, and that I hope you
have or will soon discover. I don't know how much love
you can stand; I don't know how much I can stand! But
there is a way that each of us can come to God. It might be
through being a missionary, or through the poor, through
solitude. It doesn't matter. What matters is to come alive
at some deep place in your own heart and say, "Oh Jesus!
That's *my* way." And follow it.

Stronger Than Our Past

When Maria Goretti was twelve years old she was sexual-
ly assaulted, and she was stabbed many times. For her, it
was a struggle of faith in Jesus, and she died of her
wounds.

One of the marvelous parts of the story is about the man
who killed her. He was sentenced to prison, and for thirty
years struggled with God and refused to be repentant.
Finally, he did repent and gave his life to the Lord. He was
even present at Maria's canonization! Try and imagine
what a great miracle of mercy his presence there was. He
knelt before the new picture of a saint—someone who
became a saint because she had resisted his own sexual
assault!

I don't know which is the greater miracle—Maria's resistance and her faithfulness, or the final giving in of this man, accepting his responsibility but believing that, even though he killed somebody, God forgave him. God's grace is that strong.

Grace is stronger than all the "skeletons we have in our closets." What skeletons do you have, things that, when you go to Christ in prayer, shout at you like this: "Don't you remember what you did? How can *you* try to be close to God? Don't you remember the dirty movies you went to? Don't you remember how you were sleeping around with people? Don't you remember—don't you remember all those things?" And we say, "Yeah, that's right," and we get up from our prayer and we walk away, ashamed to be in God's presence.

I often think of those moments, because I do that too—I walk away. I think of this man who had such faith in the mercy of God that he got up out of prison, walked to St. Peter's, and rejoiced and praised God for Maria's faith, and praised God for the mercy in his own life. That's how strong God is, and how strong God's grace is.

In the Old Testament, Joseph is a type of Jesus. His brothers sold him down the river. Then they came to Joseph. Joseph pretended he didn't know them, but in his heart he was just waiting to embrace them. He even went in his room and he wept—wept for the time when he could throw his arms around them and welcome them.

That is the situation of all of us with whatever "skeletons" we have. God is weeping and waiting until we come to him. It doesn't get harder for God to forgive us the greater our sins become. A man came to me once to confess that he had killed somebody. It wasn't harder to raise my hand and bless him—in fact, it was a lot easier. Forgiveness is easy for God. He's really strong and he's really merciful.

Maria came in a dream one night to the man who had killed her. She came with a bouquet of flowers. We rejoice in Maria, in her faithfulness; we thank God also for this dream that this man had. Let us have great confidence in the mercy of Jesus and not listen to all those voices within us that remind us of our past. God is stronger than our past, and greater than all our sins.

Pray For the Teachers of the Church

If I were to ask the reader if he or she had a personal devotion of some kind to St. Francis of Assisi, I imagine I would get quite a few affirmative nods of the head. If I were to ask how many had some kind of devotion to St. Thomas Aquinas, the response, I'm sure, would be quite minimal. And yet, if the question were asked, "Which of these two men had the greatest impact on the Western Church?" it would really be difficult to say. Their influences were different, to be sure, but both were vast and incalculable. Each one must examine his or her conscience as to why we lack devotion to people like Aquinas.

In every age there are thousands of people whose search for God is inexorably bound up with their search for truth, to whom as with Gandhi, Truth and God are almost synonymous. For such people, the Lord in every age graciously raises up great minds like Aquinas to meet their needs. After all, he has created and given these people a thirst for truth. It would be unfair if the Lord did not quench this thirst in the proper way.

Who can calculate the number of people down through the ages who have literally come to faith in Christ through reading someone like St. Thomas? God attracts people to his Son in many ways—through lovers like Francis, through beauties like the starry heavens, and through intellects like that of Aquinas. It is well-known that Jacques Maritain and his wife Raïssa made a suicide pact if within a year they could not find the truth. Aquinas played a significant part in their discovery. Couldn't we say that Aquinas was God's instrument for saving these two precious people for Christ's work in the modern world?

There is a great deal of disparagement of the rational mind today, and with much justification. The rational, logical, scientific mind, cut off from its roots in faith and mystery and intuition, cannot answer its own incessant questions. When St. Paul speaks about "teachers," he always mentions them in the third place, after the Apostles and Prophets, that is, after the tradition handed down and after the prophetic, intuitive voices of the community which are in religious, contemplative communion with the Spirit of God. When the mind is in subjection to these higher gifts in the community, then it can stretch and think and grasp to the farthest limits of its abilities and God-given powers. Thomas' brilliant mind *was* in subordination to the higher gifts, and so he could, without harm and in full freedom, expand the magnificent powers of his intellect. And this breadth and expansion has enraptured and enthralled the minds of thousands ever since.

Jesus gave as one of the examples of the kingdom the little mustard seed growing into a very large bush. Thomas was only five years old when he first entered the monastic schools of his day. In his mind and heart grew a great treasure of wisdom and life. What a marvelous realization of the parable of the Lord: those seeds of thought in the young Aquinas growing into such a fountain of wisdom and knowledge that still fructifies the life of the Church after many centuries.

We also know that only a few years after his death, twenty propositions in Aquinas' works were condemned by the highest doctrinal commission of the Church! Great minds are like great prophets; often unaccepted in their own times and countries because they are ahead of their times. They are often misunderstood and seen as destructive influences. But history is always the final judge.

Do you ever pray for the great minds of the Church today? We may disagree on who exactly they are, but do they figure in your prayers? Do you ever enter into the silence and intellectual combats of those who have been given the call to be teachers in the Church? They too are performing an invaluable service for the Church. Others like Mother Teresa and Dorothy Day appeal to our hearts; that is understandable. But I hope that you pray sometimes for the teachers of the Church, the theologians whose opinions sometimes you may disagree with, but whose learning and wisdom are indispensable to the Church. They too are fighting great battles on spiritual frontiers. They deserve our love, our support and our prayers.

Mary Magdalen

Sometimes I talk to the saints. I also imagine them talking back to me. That's a very good way to get to know them. Today I talked to Mary Magdalen. Among other things she said: "There's always a great deal of emphasis put on the forgiveness of my sins. Surely it *was* a very joyful occasion. But," she said, "I had seen Jesus forgiving people, and I had really *expected* that he would forgive me. Especially," she added, "since Jesus never got too upset over sexual sins. I had watched him. He got really angry with a lot of the hypocrites. But people like myself who often were weak and ignorant, well, I knew I could expect forgiveness from him."

Then she remarked: "You know what *was* unexpected, and what *was* the greatest joy of all, and that I continue to marvel at for all eternity? I never expected that he would become *my friend*.

"You know how it is with great people. You meet them, and they give you things, or grant your requests; and then you bow and leave, you know, you always do that with great people." She said, "I expected something like that from Jesus, that he would graciously forgive me and then that would be it.

"But," she said, "marvel of marvels! He really wanted to get to know me. He introduced me to his mother later on, and I began to travel around with him; I was drawn into his circle of friends. That was to me the most surprising gift of all. I never expected that. Especially with my past, I didn't feel that he would come close to the likes of me. I learned little by little in my friendship with him that he purified all my loves.

"The outstanding example of his friendship was when he came to visit me *first* after rising from the dead. For a long time I never realized that I *was* one of the first ones. But can you imagine! When friends return from a long trip, whom do they call upon first but the people that they're closest to, that they love the most. It never dawned

on me until years later that Jesus had been on his longest of
journeys, through death and back again. And when he
came back, he thought, 'Well, whom should I visit first?'
Me! Isn't that incredible! Me, the sinner! Me, the pros-
titute! It will take me all eternity to really fathom that act
of love.

"Then I began to realize that God not only loved me in
the sense of giving me things, but he allowed his own heart
to be captivated by me. *That* I never expected. I was captivated by him, but he seemed to be captivated by me also.
Now, forever and ever, I rejoice in the friendship of Jesus,
and grow deeper and deeper into an understanding of his
love."

St. John Vianney

"My ways are not your ways, and my thoughts are not
your thoughts. As high as the heavens are from the earth,
so are my thoughts above your thoughts, and my ways
above your ways."

There are a lot of evils in the world. We often look to
God and say, "God, don't you know what's going on?
Why don't you *do* something?" Often there's a great
silence. Then we wonder if God really *does* know what's
going on.

When St. John Vianney went to his little village of Ars
around 1830 or 1840, it was a spiritual disaster area.
Nobody was going to the sacraments. People were drinking like crazy. John Vianney made a pact with God. He
promised: "God, I will give my life, I will fast and pray, if
you will save my people." And God replied, "O.K., it's a
deal."

John Vianney fasted and prayed like few priests in history have fasted and prayed. He slept about an hour a day, hardly ate anything, spent many hours in the confessional serving his people. Little by little, over the years, people's hearts were changed. By the time he died, thousands of people were coming to Ars. Even today in that area of the country, people have a deep and profound faith.

In our trials we say, "God, *do* something!" And God says, "O.K., You give me your life. Let me invade your life. Let me come to the people through you and things will happen." We ask, "Can't you do it some other way! Isn't there some other way besides me giving my life?" God answers, "No, there isn't."

John Vianney had no techniques; he didn't develop a new school of mysticism. He read the Desert Fathers. The key to his life was that he had compassion on God's people. He wasn't just trying to work out his own perfection. He wasn't just trying to become holy for some reason. That's O.K. But it's not really enough. It's not deep enough. It won't last. "My life for theirs." And God saved his people.

Very simply, that's the message of his life. His pact with God really worked. The question that his life puts to us is, "How much compassion do *we* have? What will we give? How far will we go? How much will we pray? How long will we fast? How much will we love? Isn't there another way?" No, there isn't.

We have to let God invade *our* lives, and allow him to come to others through us. There is no other *real* way, no other lasting way.

"God, give us a *realistic* desire to change the world. Not

a 'pie in the sky,' not a theory that we can work out, but give us such a compassion for the world that will allow us to change our lives so that you can come to the world through us.''

That's a real desire. And if we all did that, then the world would change. We would know in our hearts how God heard our prayers and hears our thoughts. Let us pray for that true compassion so that God might work through us and transform his world.

It's the Lord!

What a wonderful model St. Peter is for responding spontaneously to the voice of Christ! When Jesus' voice came to him over the waters, he jumped in! When he saw that it was Jesus cooking breakfast on the shore, he jumped! Peter always said, ''It's the Lord! My goodness, how wonderful!''

In the Acts of the Apostles Peter also hears these same words, but in a very difficult situation. He is in danger of being arrested and perhaps being stoned to death. But Peter hears the words, ''Peter, it's me, it is the Lord, and I want you to stand up for my Name.'' In both joyful and difficult situations, Peter reacted with joy.

I want to tell you a true story that happened in a city in Russia not too long ago, in a city where liturgical ceremonies aren't permitted, and people have to worship in their homes. This little group was celebrating the Eucharist, the supper of the Lord, and they were about halfway through. Usually, if they got halfway through, the danger was past and they relaxed.

But halfway through this liturgy two soldiers of the

secret police barged in with guns. They interrupted the service and declared "Those who will renounce Christ may leave; we will deal with the others." It was the voice of the Lord saying, "It is me. Your faith in me is being challenged." Several of the people left.

As the doors closed, these two soldiers of the secret police put down their guns and said, "We are your brothers in Christ. We wanted to worship with the *real* Christians!" They were Christians who had infiltrated the secret police.

If we have really met the resurrected Jesus, whenever we hear his voice, whether it's in joyful or difficult situations, if we hear Jesus saying, "Hey, it's Me!" let us pray for each other that, like Peter, we will have the greatness of heart to respond with generosity. It may be jumping into the water, or standing up before princes and kings professing that Jesus Christ is the only name by which we can be saved. Let us pray that whenever we hear in our hearts—"It is the Lord!"—we may run to him with great enthusiasm.

Discussing Satan's Activity

When Jesus called Peter "Satan," he was speaking ironically, because he added right afterwards, "Because the way *you* think is not God's way, but man's." Our Lord wouldn't say that to Satan. He knows how Satan thinks.

Today there's really a rash of thinking about Satan, and I think that we have to be careful now about not ascribing too much to him. Jesus said to Peter: "Get behind me Satan," as Peter was thinking very devilish thoughts. It is not very clear when exactly Satan is directly involved.

Since we're always looking for a way out of our responsibilities, Satan could be a very good excuse. I take it as a rule of thumb myself that I am responsible for most of my warped desires and thoughts, and until it becomes something more obvious, I have no time to think about Satan. I'm too busy asking for mercy, and praying, and doing what I can with God's grace to overcome the inclinations. If Satan is involved in it, he'll have to make it very clear; otherwise I don't have any time for him.

Another mistake we often make about Satan is that we think there's some great battle going on between God and Satan. There's no battle going on between God and Satan. The battle is over. God is God, and Satan is Satan, and the victory is *over,* the battle is won.

It's true, there's a conflict between *us* and Satan. Sometimes we lose because we don't believe strongly enough in the victory of Christ. But the battle is over between Christ and Satan, and the victory is won. Part of the good news is that Jesus has conquered Satan.

It's also part of our faith-understanding that Satan is involved in the world and sometimes in our lives, though I think we have to be very careful in trying to pinpoint exactly when. We believe in Christ; we turn our thoughts to him. One thing we know about Satan is what Jesus told us—He said he is a liar. If you want to know what devilish thoughts are, they're thoughts that tell us that God cannot overcome the problems in us and around us. It's interesting too, the kind of devilish thoughts that Jesus pointed out to Peter. Peter wanted to have Easter without Good Friday, and Jesus commanded, "Get behind me."

Let us increase our faith in the power of Christ, increase our faith in the victory of Jesus, over all the forces that seek to destroy us or separate us from him. Let us pray too, that we might have the gift of discernment, and that we keep the proper perspective about the sources of difficulty in our lives.

Now They Know

When we think of the saints we think, of course, of the known ones, those whose feasts we celebrate all year long. But when I was praying the Office this morning I came across this line: "He who keeps his pledge, come what may, who takes no interest on a loan and accepts no bribes against the innocent, such a man will stand firm forever." When I read that line I stopped and I thought of all the *unknown* people in heaven. I thought that I would draw your attention to the millions and millions of people who are with God, who are unknown to us. Untold millions see now that God is faithful to them.

At the charismatic conference in Kansas City, one of the lines that set the whole convention into pandemonium was: "You know, if you take a peek at the back of the Book, Jesus wins." There's so much pain and suffering in the world; the drama of life is only half over. God is not totally glorified here on earth, but we will see him glorified one day. God cannot be conquered; God is going to win.

Jesus said, "Blessed are the poor." Think, my brothers and sisters, of all the deceased poor of all the ages of the world. The poor of Africa, the teeming poor of India, the poor of the modern ghetto. Millions and millions of people. All these poor now know that God is God, and that he is faithful to his promises.

Jesus said, "Happy the gentle." Think, my brothers and

sisters, of the countless gentle hearts down through the ages of the world, people that opted for gentleness instead of power. It wasn't clear to them whether God would help them, or whether their gentleness would really be greater than power. But now they know. They know that God is faithful to his promises and they're glad they were faithful to their gentle hearts.

Jesus said, "Happy those who mourn." Think of all the tears, my brothers and sisters, that have been shed throughout all the centuries of the world. God promised that he would dry every one of them. God will comfort all the tears of the world. Oceans and oceans of tears. And now they know. All these people know that God is love and is faithful to his promises, that he dries all tears.

Jesus said, "Happy those who hunger and thirst for what is right." Think of the millions of people who had this instinct in their hearts for justice and doing the right thing. They found out there were people who were crushing other people, who were hungry for power and domination. They didn't follow them but trusted the instinct of their heart for justice and right. They weren't sure that God would ever see, that God would hear their plea, that God loved them. But now they know. All these people who trusted their deepest instinct know that God is God, and that God is faithful.

Jesus said, "Blessed are the merciful." Those who didn't fight back. Those who didn't throw rocks when somebody else threw a rock at them. The merciful—those who did turn the other cheek often; who began to wonder about this and did not understand the instinct to refrain. Now they know that God is mercy and that he is faithful to his promises.

"Happy the pure of heart." Happy those who believed

in love, that love is the deepest thing. They knew that in the end we would be judged on love. Their life wasn't easy. They saw people who hate; they saw them making money; they saw them gaining all the positions in the world. And they wondered: "Does God see? Does God understand? Is God love?" They were faithful to love and now they know. Now they see that God *is* God, and that God is love, and that love is stronger than hate.

Jesus said, "Happy those who try to make peace." Those who make war control the world. Peacemakers wonder: "Is it worthwhile to make peace? Maybe we should make war too." But no. They were faithful to their instinct for peace. And now they know. Now they know that the peacemakers are blessed and that yes, God is faithful and that God is peace and love.

I had this vision of millions and millions of unknown people who followed the deepest thing in their hearts, and who now know that God is true, and that God is on their side.

My brothers and sisters, we should keep this vision in mind. In our own lives we often wonder if we should switch gears and fight. Maybe the powerful people are right after all. But gone before us are millions of holy people who were faithful to the end to all the deepest instincts of their hearts. And now they know. We rejoice with all these people. We pray for one another that we too are faithful to what we know is really *God* in our hearts.

The Party Is the Blind

I have been privileged the past two years to be with our Applicants as they study and reflect on Catherine's spirituality in the Little Mandate. (The Applicants are those who are seriously praying and thinking about joining our Madonna House family.) It's been a very real grace for me. I feel the Lord has helped me to understand a little bit better the spirituality that he has given us through Catherine.

There is a passage in the Gospel about inviting the poor and the crippled and the lame to your banquet. This is very much at the heart of our spiritual life, because it is at the heart of the Gospel.

Catherine, many years ago, heard Jesus say to her: "Come and stay here with me with the poor. Come into the marketplace and be with me. I am lonely." Many years ago she wrote that the essence of our Apostolate is somehow to assuage the loneliness of Christ. In one real sense, each part of our Mandate could be understood as helping us to go on the long, immense journey into the hearts of the poor and the crippled and the lame—first of all, of ourselves, and then, of all those who cross our path in life.

Our Mandate says: "Little, be always little." That's so we're able to bend low in our hearts, so that there is nobody on the face of the earth before whom we cannot bow down and serve. There are so many things in our hearts that are exalted and proud and that seek the first places. "Be little" for us means to bend low, as low as we can, so that there is no one we cannot approach.

"Do little things exceedingly well." Do everything with love and handle everything with gentleness so that when we meet people, we will handle them with gentleness as well.

"Pray." As Catherine says, prayer is listening to the heartbeats of God. Pray. Listen to the heartbeats of God, and you will be able to listen to the heartbeats of the poor and the crippled and the lame.

"Fast." Realize your total dependence on God, how needy you are, so that you will be sensitive to the needs of everybody else.

"Be hidden." Be hidden because the poor and the crippled and the lame are often hidden and they are often shy and hesitant. We have to know how to be hidden and to be present to them in a simple way, like Jesus, who was God present to us.

"Go into the depths of men's hearts." Yes, undertake that long journey. Jesus took the long journey from his Father to us and we are to take that long journey into the heart of one another.

My brothers and sisters, Jesus says, "Don't arrange private little parties for yourselves." He doesn't mean that sometimes we can't be with our friends; he was often alone with his friends. He means that we are all somehow preparing for the great banquet that his Father has for everybody, and we can't settle down into any little parties until all the preparations are made. The "parties" are all those places in our hearts where we say, "I want to be just where I am and nobody else, please, come in. I have enough, I am sufficient, nobody else enter, please."

Jesus tells us, "Don't do that. The party is precisely allowing the poor and the crippled and the lame to come into our hearts." In our present situation, *that* is the party, *that* is the supper. When we are preparing to get together with our friends, and a stranger comes, we say, "Oh, there it goes." We were going to have an intimate gathering with our friends and somebody crippled comes, somebody lonely, somebody lame. And we complain, "There goes the party!" Jesus says, "That's not true. The party and the supper *for God* is *saving his people."* That's what all parties are for; that's what all the little gatherings are for; that's what all the preparations are for.

In some real sense, we can't ever celebrate here completely because there are so many people who don't know Jesus, who don't know about the supper, who don't know the Gospel. There's something missing in our celebrations. The preparations are incomplete.

Very simply, that's the word that I would like to share with you: in Jesus' eyes, the party *is* the blind, the party *is* the crippled, the party *is* the lame. We have to enter more and more deeply into that to see the joy that God experiences when people come to life and are saved. That's the supper! That's the celebration!

Always remember that we're preparing to enter into the hearts of all those who don't know Jesus so that one day we can all celebrate on Mount Zion together.

I Promise

I recently renewed my promises in the Madonna House family. It made me reflect on just exactly what I was promising. I had been asking the Lord, saying, "Teach me exactly what I am promising."

One of the themes that constantly recurs in Scripture is the Lord saying, "I will be with you." "God is with us." Our faith and understanding is that God is faithful to his promises to us. What did he promise? He promised that he would always be with us. During Advent we think of the times when, for thousands of years, people waited. God promised to come to them, and he came. He was faithful to his word.

What am *I* promising? To follow Jesus. Well, I've been promising to follow Jesus for a long time, and I hope I always will. What am I promising that's new? To live the way of life in Madonna House? I think that's close to what I'm promising.

Catherine says in our *Way of Life* that "The essence of our Apostolate is to love one another." I'm saying, "I promise to help this family grow in love. I promise to help this family live the Gospel better. I promise to share with them my own journey to Christ. I promise that I will try and love them, even if they fail to live the Gospel, or they fail in love, that won't matter. I will still love them, and I will stay with them. God made a covenant with us and stuck with us."

I'm promising that I will no longer say, "What does God want from *me?*" but, "What does God want from us?" I'm promising that I will no longer see my life in individual terms—"What is the Holy Spirit leading *me* to do?" But—"What is the Holy Spirit leading me to do in context of my family, my loved ones?"

I'm not simply promising to hang on for dear life and hoping that everything turns out for the good. I'm promising to try to make our life more conformable to the Gospel, more in God. I promise to try and make it an exciting life, a life of love.

In short, I am promising to bind up my life inextricably with those of my family. I promise to stay with them no matter what. I believe I can do this in the strength of him who promised and stayed with us, no matter what.

Seeking What Was Lost

God has come in search of men. When we were wandering around in darkness, Jesus, the Good Shepherd, came in search of us to lead us back to his Father. Jesus has released among us this same power of concern and shepherding of each other. Now he uses us to reach other people, those who are really in need and who are wandering around in the wastelands.

About eight years ago I was in a parish. One morning about eight o'clock, I was in the office doing some paperwork. The pastor came in. He was vested for Mass and was just about to go out. He brought in with him a very distraught man—Tom, we'll call him. He asked me to take care of him since he couldn't at this time. Tom came in. He was very obviously in a state of shock. He kept mumbling something like, "I killed her. I killed her. God, why couldn't it have been me? There's no sense living. What's the use of it all!"

He went on and on like this for about ten or fifteen minutes. Then he suddenly said, "I'm going for a walk." I didn't think that was such a good idea. So I suggested going for a ride. We rode for a couple of hours. In the course of the ride and conversation he told me that he had just been involved in a shooting, and that he had killed somebody, and that he was being sought after by the police. He had run away, hitchhiked, and the driver had dropped him off in front of the church; he had decided to come in.

Sure enough, we turned on the radio and we heard the account of the shooting. We stopped to get a morning paper and on the headlines was the account of the shooting and his name and they were looking for him.

Tom wasn't really running. He was going to give himself up. But he just needed time to get himself together. He didn't see any reason for living. It was the end of the road. The woman he killed he evidently really had loved. He claimed it was an accident. He was going to shoot himself but she had grabbed the gun and it went off and she was killed. For him that was the end of life. He was thirty-one years old and there was no reason to keep living.

About one o'clock in the afternoon he called the jail downtown. We went together and he turned himself in.

Over a series of weeks and months I went back to visit him and tried to say things like, "You're a young person," and "Who knows what the future holds?" I forget what I said. During that time he was also allowed to go out during the day. We used to go swimming together. We used to go out for a beer. We used to just talk. About a year ago I had to go back to testify at his trial. Tom was sentenced to twelve years in Attica for second degree manslaughter. He's appealing the case right now and it looks pretty good because the evidence was very tenuous against him; it looks very good for a revision of his case.

During this past year the tone of his letters began to change. He started to joke, and there was much more hope in his life. I want to read you what he wrote to me a few months ago:

'. . . So from all indications, it looks good. If everything turns out the way it looks it will, I want you to know it's because you and only you helped me when I was lost. This may sound strange to you, but I am still lost to a degree. However I know I am on the road to recovery, both mentally and in spirit.'

For me, this was like someone coming back from the dead!

At each Eucharist we celebrate the mystery of Christ's power among us: Jesus, who sought us out, works through us to lead others back to hope and back to real life. Let us pray for each other that we never turn our backs on anybody who really needs our help, that we always keep in mind what Jesus did for us: When we were lost, when we were without hope, he came after us and led us back to a new day.

The Lord also taught me something else through all this. As the weeks and months of my relationship with Tom went on, I found that he was becoming *my friend.* It was a very strange thing. When people come to you, you have a tendency to look at them as clients or patients or cases. But as I visited him, and as we went out and did things, it began to dawn on me that we were becoming friends. The Lord had taught me that if we really want to be involved in healing others, we have to become their friends, like Jesus became our friend. He taught me that friendship takes time, that we have to be with people whether it's in jail or wherever their situation happens to be.

I thank God for his coming in search of me, and pray that in his strength I may go in search of others and continue the shepherding mission of Jesus among us.

Only God Makes Things Grow

In our practical, everyday life we often live and act under the illusion that *we* make things grow. This is so because we can certainly decide upon and initiate projects—in short, make things *happen.* This is not the same as making things grow. Only God can make things grow, because real growth takes place at the level of microcosmic gradations guided by wisdom. For a person to live at this level, either for himself or herself or in his or her relations with others, it requires the gifts of truth and love which only flow from the Spirit.

The image or model we have in our minds of how things grow is extremely important then. It is important for us, since we must constantly make decisions to become what the Lord envisions us to be. It is important in our God-given work, because we must decide what will be the best way to foster personal, familial, cultural, or any other kind of growth for which we are responsible. When you really think about it, we are constantly making decisions which deal precisely with the becoming of all things. But all becoming is not necessarily growth. "How do things grow?" is an extremely important question.

I believe the best model for growth is nature, and I think it is the model most used in Scripture to explain how people grow. In the very first psalm the just man is likened to a "tree that is planted by water streams, yielding its fruit in due season" (Ps. 1:3). In Psalm 91 we read: "The just will flourish like the palm tree, and grow like a Lebanon cedar" (Ps. 91:13). "I will fall like dew on Israel, he shall bloom like the lily" (Hos. 14:6). Then there are the familiar parables of Jesus about the word of God which grows like a seed (Lk. 8:11-15), the kingdom which also grows like a seed (Mt. 13:31), and the wheat and the darnel used as images of the good and the bad (Mt. 13:24-30).

Among the many effects of sin is the distortion of the growth process. We could approach this distortion from many different angles, but the Epistle to the Ephesians gives us a key: "If we live by the *truth* and in *love,* we shall grow in all ways into Christ" (4:16).

The basic truth about all real growth is that it is gradual and at a level we have difficulty being aware of. Did you ever sit and try to watch a flower grow or the sun rise, little by little? Because we can envision with our minds the goal toward which the growth is tending, we become impatient. Impatience makes us race over the necessary intermediate steps. In thus running ahead of God, we make things *happen,* but we are not necessarily assisting God in true growth. True growth demands humility—the patience to let everything grow little by little, since this is the only way it can.

Love, in this growth context, means reaching out toward the things which will bring us to our goal as envisioned by God. "Go on growing in the grace and knowledge of our Lord and Savior Jesus Christ" (2 Pet. 3:13). Reaching out toward Christ, and to everything in keeping with the mind of Christ, is true growth. Jesus himself, the power and the wisdom to reach out toward him, and the humility to feel our way toward him one step at a time—all these are gifts of God. This is why only God can make things grow. God is the source of this creative transformation process; our task is to help plant and water (1 Cor. 3:6). Such love and truth is the "spiritual honesty," the "pure milk of the Spirit to make you grow unto salvation" (1 Pet. 2:2).

The Lines That Give Beauty

Here in the poustinia I often ask myself, "What does our dedication say to our friends who are here, or to those who come to visit us? What are we saying to them? People may see us trying to keep the laws of God. The words "commandments" and "law" strike very hard on our ears; they sound like very confining things. But for the people of the Bible, God's law was the *blueprint of freedom.* God's word told them how to live and what to do with their lives. One of the problems of modern man, the problem of the philosopher Sartre, for example, is that he experiences that he is free, but free for what? That's the problem. What are we supposed to do with our freedom? We believe that God's word is the blueprint of liberation. That's why the psalmist sings about God's word as being a joy to his heart, because it tells him what to do and how to live and how to get back to God.

Some people might think that promising things like poverty and chastity and obedience is limiting our lives. But we say it's limiting in the same way that an artist's hand is limited when he draws a picture. He no longer splashes paint all over the wall. He draws lines and makes beautiful images. And if that's what you mean by limitation, then yes, we are limiting our lives that way. We are painting a beautiful picture with our choices. It's limitation in the same way that a sculptor is limiting the marble with his hammer and chisel, making a beautiful sculpture. We don't say he's limiting his strokes. No, he's just not chipping away haphazardly. He's very precise, and he's making his strokes very neatly, and the result is a beautiful statue. If that's what people mean by limitation, then we plead guilty to limitation, because we see our choices as the lines that give beauty to our lives.

We certainly don't say that Madonna House is the only way to be a Christian, to live the Christian life. But we say it's one way, it's our way, and we have chosen it, and it's "something beautiful for God." It's not everything—all possible values—but we believe in some way we can achieve everything that Christ wants us to become by this particular choice.

The second thing we might say to people who see us from the outside, who visit us, is contained in what Paul says: "The Jews look for miracles and wonders, and the Greeks look for wisdom, but we preach a crucified Christ." The Jew and the Greek are symbols; they are types of mentalities that look for ways to heal the world. Some people are Greeks in the sense that they think knowledge is going to save them: "If only we had enough knowledge, we could heal the ills of mankind." But never before has man had so much knowledge and known so little what to do with it.

There's another type of person who is expecting a miraculous cure just around the corner, something that will fall from the stars, a wonder, a miracle cure that will solve everything. To these and other kinds of saviors of the world, we say that we have chosen Jesus crucified and risen from the dead. We cannot avoid suffering and pain, poverty and limitation. If we bear these things with the Spirit of Jesus, we come to true joy and we touch life at its deepest.

Finally, we try to say that the love of Christ is strong. There is a lot of talk about love in the world, a wishy-washy type of love. It doesn't make strong decisions; it doesn't know what to choose. Jesus has given us the power to see clearly what life is about, and we choose it. Sometimes people criticize us and those like us who have chosen such a stance. But if you ask them, "Well, what have *you* chosen?" they often haven't chosen anything because they don't know what to choose or whom to follow, or they don't have the strength to make a strong choice. We say that the Word of God is a light for our feet and a lamp for our minds and that Jesus has given us his Spirit to choose and to love and to say, "This is where we stand and we know where we are going."

Mary was the first one who saw the new plan of God—that life comes through death. Even when Jesus had died and no one else was around, Mary was the only person who believed in her heart that somehow, through the death of her Son, new life was springing up on the earth. And so, as we choose what seems to be a most difficult way of life, Mary is our model. We ask her to pray for us and to give us the same understanding and love that she had. For the meaning of life is not in the wonders of the Jews or the wisdom of the Greeks. It's in Jesus crucified, who is the Wisdom of God and the Power of God.

President Kennedy, at the end of his inaugural speech, addressed the whole world rather dramatically when he said, "Let anyone who can hear, hear (I forget his exact words). For the cause of freedom we are willing to cross any ocean, and bear any burden." I feel like saying something like that: "Let anybody who wants to listen, wherever they are, hear this: we have chosen Jesus, and we are willing to bear any burden and cross any ocean, that his life might enter the world through us."

Even as I say that, I know that our hearts are weak and that we will fall, but we know that Jesus knows that too. In the Gospel he says that "He knows what's in man." He understands us. But we pray that in spite of our weakness, he will use us—use us for the healing of the world. We believe that together, living in the Spirit of Jesus, we can go back to the Father, and we can take an awful lot of people with us!